THE
MUSICAL
MILKMAN
MURDER

Quentin Falk is a veteran film journalist and critic. He is also the author of books on Alfred Hitchcock, Anthony Hopkins, Albert Finney, Lord Lew Grade, The Rank Organisation, and Graham Greene, which was short-listed for the Mobil/bfi Film Book of the Year Award.

THE MUSICAL MILKMAN MURDER

IN THE IDYLLIC COUNTRY VILLAGE USED TO FILM
MIDSOMER MURDERS, IT WAS THE REAL-LIFE MURDER
STORY THAT SHOCKED 1920 BRITAIN

QUENTIN FALK

JOHN BLAKE

Published by John Blake Publishing Ltd,
3 Bramber Court, 2 Bramber Road,
London W14 9PB, England

www.johnblakepublishing.co.uk

www.facebook.com/Johnblakepub facebook
twitter.com/johnblakepub twitter

First published in paperback in 2012

ISBN: 978 1 85782 807 8

British Library Cataloguing-in-Publication Data:

A catalogue record for this book is available from the British Library.

Design by www.envydesign.co.uk

Printed and bound in Great Britain by CPI Group (UK) Ltd

1 3 5 7 9 10 8 6 4 2

Papers used by John Blake Publishing are natural, recyclable products made
from wood grown in sustainable forests. The manufacturing processes
conform to the environmental regulations of the country of origin.

Every attempt has been made to contact the relevant copyright-holders,
but some were unobtainable. We would be grateful if the
appropriate people could contact us.

To Hollie and Bernard

Contents

INTRODUCTION

This story, as so many stories often do, began – or, more properly, first took shape – in the manner of a Chinese whisper, when you aren't quite sure whether its repetition is an accurate account of the original telling or else just an increasingly mangled version of that initial truth.

When my father bought back Old Barn Cottage in 1966 after it had been out of the family for 23 years, I was vaguely aware of some of its dim, distant history known locally, and lip-smackingly, as 'The Musical Milkman Murder'. But who murdered whom – was the milkman the murderer or the victim? I didn't know and wasn't even particularly concerned to discover at the time.

All I think I knew then was that the killing – whether by axe, shotgun, strangulation or poisoning – apparently occurred a couple of years before my paternal grandfather,

Lionel, had first purchased the place, then known as plain Barn Cottage (he later added the 'Old') for £700 as a weekend retreat from the family's North London home in 1923, before selling it in 1943 (for £1,800), at the height of the Second World War.

Our first real inkling of its infamous past came in the very early 1970s when some neighbours spotted a middle-aged woman standing outside the gate looking at the place with sad eyes. They approached her discreetly and helpfully informed her that none of the family who owned the property was currently in residence. They then enquired why she was staring so intently at the rose-covered cottage, a pretty cliché of Buckinghamshire brick-and-flint, adorned with gables and criss-crossing Elizabethan timbers, dating originally from the turn of the 17th century.

She told them that, years ago, there had been a murder there. Yes, they replied, they knew of it, although they didn't have any of the real facts of the case to pass on to her. Then, to their stunned surprise – and later ours when the news was relayed to my father and his family – she told them that her father, the milkman, had murdered her mother Kate, and that she, Hollie, just two at the time, was their surviving child. More shockingly, Hollie – probably aged about 54 as she revealed all this to our increasingly astonished neighbours – then told them that she'd only very recently discovered the terrible truth about her dead parents via an anonymous call.

Growing up first with her father's sister and then with her paternal grandmother, she had always been fobbed off whenever the question of her parentage arose. All she had been told was that they had 'died from the fever'. She remembered vividly once asking her aunt whom she was most like – her father or her mother? 'Your father,' came the chilly reply. End of conversation.

When, following the stark revelation about her parents, further elements of the truth began to filter out – that Hollie had been born in the infirmary of Winchester Prison, the possibility of a botched suicide pact, and so on – Hollie, by now on her third marriage and the mother of five children, as well as grandmother of increasingly more over the succeeding years, wanted finally, desperately, to nail down the real facts of the case. Her first port of call – after first making contact with Births, Marriages and Deaths at Somerset House – simply enough, was the location of the final resting places of her father and mother.

To Mrs Hollie D from the Governor of HM Prison, Oxford, 10 September 1973:

Dear Madam,
Thank you for your letter of 9 September. It is confirmed that a George Arthur Bailey was executed and buried at this prison. As regards your mother, I am unable to assist you. I advise you to write to the Registrar of Births and Deaths, Somerset House, London WC2 to find out the date of death and the parish in which she was buried and using this information to write to the Vicar of the parish concerned for information regarding the location of the grave.

Two days later, the Governor of Oxford Prison wrote again to Hollie in response to a note the day before asking if she could visit his grave: 'Thank you for your letter of 11 September … I am sorry that it is not possible to allow visits to graves in the prison. I hope you are successful in tracing your mother's grave.'

Whether she was pointed in the right direction by Somerset House, one doesn't know, but, on 26 September, she wrote to Buckinghamshire County Council for information and received an extremely swift response from the Superintendent Registrar referring her next to the local vicar at Little Marlow – and he even enclosed a stamped, addressed envelope for the cleric to reply.

On 11 October, she received the following from Rev John Crawford, Curate of St John the Baptist, Little Marlow: 'Thank you for your letter. The number of your mother's grave in Little Marlow Cemetery is No 256; burial on 6 October 1920. The numbers are all lost or misplaced so it would be hard to locate but it is in the oldest part facing the chapel door. Wishing you every blessing in the future.'

In November, she wrote to the Editor of the *News of the World*, Cyril Lear, asking if he had any back copies of the paper for 1920, the year of the murder. Her approach to the paper specifically may have been to do with the possibility that the anonymous tip-off about her parentage had originated from that now defunct Sunday newspaper. He politely replied that he couldn't help but suggested instead that she contact the Newspaper Library at Colindale, which continues to store a remarkable collection of national and regional newspapers.

The trail then ran cold, it seems, until it became apparent, in March 1974, that Hollie had made contact with my father, eight years after he bought back Old Barn Cottage; she had sent him what few bits of documentation about the case she'd managed to track down. He invited her to tour the cottage properly and she sent him this letter, after her visit, on 29 March:

We were very pleased to meet you, and thank you for your kindness in letting us look over the cottage. I felt no sadness. I was three years old two days after my mother was buried. I always wanted to know where my mother was buried; as you can see, I only found out last year. My father's mother brought me up. I was brought up to believe that it was meant to be a triple suicide, but my father lost his nerve and it was only my mother that died. I know he was hung at Oxford Prison. I excepted [sic] that. My grandmother died when I was nearly 17 years old. I was left to make my own life. When I received my mother's death certificate last year, I knew there was more than I had been told. When I wrote away to the London Library and received the papers, I was shattered. My tears were for my poor mother, only 22 years old and 7 months pregnant …

Hollie then concluded her letter by also thanking my father for his offer to her of a 'job looking after the cottage … but my husband's job has a pension at the end of his retirement. But I will certainly keep a look out for someone for you.' This came as a huge and somewhat unsettling surprise to me; my father had never told me of this in his lifetime (he died in 1997 aged 86), and I hadn't seen the reference until I started researching this book. This was the same year I had moved into the property full time, after the place had been, for the most part, a family bolt-hole for weekends and holidays since 1966.

A month after her visit, my father wrote to Tony Church, Editor of the *Bucks Free Press*, the most widely circulated local paper, asking if it would be possible to obtain copies of the contemporary coverage of the case and the trial in 1921. Church replied: 'With reference to the Bailey murder at Little

Marlow, back in 1920, I recall that we did have an enquiry from the daughter some months ago and that from the rather vague details she had we were able to trace the report of the murder and the subsequent trial proceedings and that we were able to give her information that has obviously led her to make the rather melancholy visit to Little Marlow. But, as you say, no doubt it has helped her to lay a ghost.'

In due course, whether via the *BFP* or the Newspaper Library, a full set of *Bucks Free Press* reports came into our family's possession before being rolled up into a tube and forgotten for another 30 years or so.

At the beginning of 1975 – and a month before I got married – Hollie wrote again to my father, reflecting, 'It has been a very depressing kind of year for me. If only I had known when I was younger, perhaps I could have forgotten it better. As it is, I shall never be able to forget. Perhaps time will help. I can only think my father was a psychopath.'

She then went on, 'The last time I visited the grave, there was a notice board up by the plot of ground where my mother is buried saying that in September this year they are going to level the graves over and, if anyone is interested, to get in touch with the council concerned. I have given it a lot of thought, and think the best thing I can do is to let them level the grave over, and let things be forgotten, or try to. I shall visit the grave once more.'

My father wrote back to Hollie two days later, on 9 January, sympathising about her 'horrible year' before telling her that the cottage was soon to become a lovely, permanent home for the happy couple – 'I only wish that your associations with it were happier. You know that there will always be a welcome for you should you come to the village and provided you give us a little bit of notice so that we are sure to be there.' That was his last ever direct communication with her.

However, nearly ten years on, in 1984, in response to a request by the *Midweek* edition of the *Bucks Free Press*, which felt the case was worth revisiting all these years later, my wife and I, now parents of two young children, took 66-year-old Hollie on a tour of the much-refurbished and considerably re-jigged cottage, certainly compared with the 1920 version or even, for that matter, the one my father had walked her round a decade before.

On, quite inappropriately, Valentine's Day, *Midweek* published a lavishly illustrated account of her visit to the cottage and the cemetery written by its chief reporter, Bob Perrin, under the cheerful headline: 'A WOMAN ORPHANED BY THE HANGMAN'S NOOSE LEARNS THE AWFUL TRUTH ABOUT HER GRUESOME CHILDHOOD'. Perrin's colourful three-page spread was followed up two years later by a chapter in his book *No Fear Nor Favour!*, re-treading some of the juiciest stories that had been carried in the *Bucks Free Press* since it was first published in early Victorian times. In among the 16 chapters, ranging, with alliterative abandon, from 'Of Fish, Riot, Rags and Rabies' to 'Of Parrots, Pubs and Punting Pleasures', was one entitled, much more succinctly, 'Of a Musical Milkman and Murder Most Foul'.

However, neither Perrin's 1984 report nor his more fleshed-out follow-up in 1986 – by which time Hollie had married for the fourth and final time – came even close to telling the whole, extraordinary story of a humble dairyman of musical ambitions with, on the face of it, homicidal tendencies. I would later begin to uncover the truth in much greater detail after I decided to take a look again at that tube of press cuttings, which had been gathering dust for years in a corner of the cottage.

As if Bailey's own background story wasn't fascinating enough, there was his sensational murder trial, historic for being the first in Britain ever to feature women jurors. Then, throughout this tale there was a recurring, eerie suicide motif. This theme of self-destruction would extend, I'd learn, after hours of digging through the Home Office file and related papers at the National Archives, to the Judge, the hangman and the Prosecution's most distinguished expert witness. The Musical Milkman cast a long shadow.

Perrin did, however, note perceptively that there was a singular irony in the site of Kate's unmarked grave. For, interred just a few strides away with an altogether more lavish memorial, was one of the world's greatest and most prolific crime writers, Edgar Wallace, who had died a dozen years after the murder.

What Perrin wouldn't have known was that, long after he resurrected the case for mostly local consumption, Little Marlow would become a fashionable location for filming top-rated television crime shows like *Inspector Morse*, *Miss Marple*, *The Inspector Lynley Mysteries* and, most prolifically – on one occasion even inside Old Barn Cottage itself – the ever popular *Midsomer Murders*. The Musical Milkman Murder was, however, a real-life slaying that would have taxed the imagination of even the most inventive TV screenwriter.

1

MURDER MOST FOUL

The year 1920 was a very good year for murder and murderers. A seven-year high of 313 'homicides' – the official Home Office catch-all term for murder, manslaughter and infanticide – was reported that year in the UK. It was a figure that, apart from another brief peak in 1925, would remain unsurpassed until the depth of the Depression in the early 1930s.

Less than two years after the November Armistice, as the country was still painfully trying to come to terms with the legalised slaughter of the Great War, in which two-and-a-half million Britons had either been killed or wounded, and the subsequent onset of a catastrophic 'flu epidemic that would claim millions more, 'foul play' came in many and all kinds of heinous guises.

In January 1920, farm labourer Edward Burrows, a convicted bigamist, took his mistress Hannah Calladine and their year-old son out on to the moors near Glossop in Derbyshire, murdered them and threw the bodies down the air-shaft of a disused mine. The next day he returned, this time disposing of Hannah's four-year-old daughter in the same place.

In August, the body of 17-year-old typist Irene Munroe was found buried in the shingle at the Crumbles near Eastbourne. It transpired that Munroe, on holiday at the coast, had been savagely beaten to death by Jack Alfred Field and William Thomas Gray, a pair of ex-Servicemen in their twenties, after she tried to resist their sexual advances.

A month before that, at Hay-on-Wye, the sleepy heart of Welsh border country, Herbert Rowse Armstrong, a diminutive, small-town solicitor and retired British Army major, poisoned his hen-pecking wife Katharine to an agonising death by arsenic.

All four killers were eventually caught, tried and hanged.

Then, on 17 September 1920, 32-year-old dairyman George Arthur Bailey, his heavily pregnant wife Kate – ten years his junior – and their two-year-old daughter Hollie, moved into Barn Cottage, Little Marlow, about half a mile up from the Thames in South Bucks, after paying in advance a month's rent of £6.

Just over a fortnight later, on 2 October, Kate was found dead by police, her body wrapped in a sheet beneath a camp bed that had been draped with a large counterpane in an upstairs bedroom of the quaint Elizabethan cottage, which had once been a thriving village bakery. From the discoloured state of the corpse, clad in a nightdress and woollen undergarments, it was evident she had been dead a few days. There was no sign of Bailey or the child.

Five months earlier, towards the end of May, Edwin Hall,

who ran a dairy in Bourne End (a small town also bordering the Thames, about a mile-and-a-half east of Little Marlow), placed an advertisement in the *Farmer and Stockbreeder* for a milk roundsman. Soon after he received a telegram from a George Bailey indicating he was 'suited' to the job. Hall then telegraphed Bailey at the address in Swindon requesting more information and, less than a week later, received the following letter, dated 27 May:

> *I have pleasure in stating that I have the qualification as in advertisement. I am abstemious, steady, energetic, of decent appearance, also a thorough milker, if required … Married, one child, with a life's experience in the dairy trade, retail and producing. I am desirous of finding a good situation, one that will be permanent for years, everything being satisfactory. My experience covers Devon and Cornish resorts, provincial towns and London … Respecting the wages required, sir, that, I think, is best left to you, as so much depends on local conditions now, with which you are more familiar than I am, and as to whether you pay an inclusive wage for honest, persevering work, or on a commission basis for new trade. I think the money question, sir, can be safely left for mutual settlement as far as I am concerned. I am free to take up my duties at any time, sir, or to come and see you, and you may depend on my efforts to further your business and to endeavour to give you complete satisfaction. Trusting to hear favourably from you, I am, sir, yours faithfully, GA Bailey.*

They met up a couple of days later in Wallingford, about halfway between Swindon and Bourne End, and Hall was so impressed with Bailey that he hired him right away at £3 a week with the promise of commission.

Just after Whitsun, on 2 June, Bailey left his sister Helen and her husband Jim Jennings' house in Swindon where he'd been living with Kate and Hollie, and moved into a small, two-storey, semi-detached house called 'Millbrook' in Bourne End, owned by Miss Mary Hillary, who lived nearby. The plan was for Kate and Hollie to remain in Wiltshire until Bailey had found his feet in Buckinghamshire.

At first, he lived in Millbrook with two or three other lodgers before, in July, writing to ask if he could rent the whole place furnished because he now wanted Kate and Hollie to join him. Also, would Miss Hillary object, he wrote, if they shared with another couple called Roper who had two children? She would say later she was surprised by this as she thought he had wanted to live there alone for a while, the arrangement being that he'd have it for at least three months before deciding whether to take it for longer.

It seems that he was an instant success after taking over a round – consisting of some 300 customers in Bourne End and adjoining Wooburn Green – that Hall would admit later was quite 'difficult'. About six hours in duration, Bailey started at 6.30 in the morning and finished around 12.30pm, after which he'd have to clean the churns and various utensils in the dairy. Boosting milk sales as well as those of butter and eggs, the persuasive Bailey was soon on an extra 5s a week with the promise from Hall that he might well get another rise in three months' time. A short, stocky man with dark hair, Bailey, who quickly became popular with his customers, could often be heard whistling or humming while doing his round, with the result that he soon earned the nickname, 'the Musical Milkman', or, just occasionally, 'The Whistling Milkman'.

What those customers didn't know at the time was that Bailey had, he would proclaim, authentic music ambitions, which were first revealed, albeit cryptically, in an advertisement he placed in the *Bucks Free Press* on 25 June. It read:

Young Lady, refined, educated, musical ability essential, required to help originator copy manuscript proof sheets and assist in development of propaganda. Pleasant, unique work; light hours. Salary, Five Guineas weekly to right person – Write, G.A.B. Free Press Office, Wycombe.

He believed he had invented a new system of musical notation that would, he hoped, simplify the teaching and the playing of music which would then prove, eventually, not only remunerative to pupils, and possibly aspiring concert pianists, but also, of course, to him.

The ad attracted a number of applicants from Marlow, Bourne End and High Wycombe, as did a follow-up two months later in the same paper. That second ad was, to say the least, rather more graphic, not to say distinctly more suspect in its content:

Young ladies, not under 16, must be over 5ft 6in, well-built, full figure or slim build. Applicants below height specified, please state qualifications as to appearance, etc. Required for highly specialised work, indoors or out. Applications from all classes entertained, as duties will be taught. – Write, in first instance, to "Snap", Free Press Office, Wycombe.

The applicants – young ladies in their late teens or very early twenties – like Winifred Field, Gladys Edwards, Lilian Marks, Mabel Tubb, Ethel Rouse and Violet Baker – flocked to Millbrook during August and early September to be given the once-over by Bailey and, in certain cases, promises of paid work that might require occasional sleepovers. The mothers of Ethel and Violet decided they needed to check out Bailey for themselves and came to Bourne End for a meeting. Mrs Rouse wanted to know why he was going to provide her daughter with a costume. He told her that, as he planned to have 40 girls working for him, he wanted them to be alike and look smart to advertise his music. She expressed her concern to him that these would be young women in his care and that she didn't want anything to happen that might blight their young lives. He assured her, 'There are some very funny things happening nowadays, but it will be quite all right.'

This human traffic to Millbrook was noted at the time by the local Bourne End bobby, PC John Gray, who would later say that after being given official instructions to keep a watch on the house – presumably the advertisements had become rather notorious locally and Bailey was, after all, an increasingly well-known character in the district – he saw as many as 30 different young women visit the place, usually between 5.00 and 8.00 in the evening.

However, there was soon a major glitch in Bailey's living arrangements and potential base for his future musical operations. On 22 July, by which time Kate, a tiny, timid-looking woman, and Hollie had joined Bailey at Millbrook, Miss Hillary wrote to him saying she wasn't willing to let the house to him any longer than the stipulated time – three months. In fact, she added, she'd like his tenancy to terminate sooner than that if possible; this similarly extended to Mr and Mrs Roper, as she'd been totally unaware of Bailey's intention to sub-let to them.

When she and Bailey met two days earlier, he had complained about the rent. This galled Miss Hillary who, in her letter wrote: 'As to the "exorbitant price" you are paying for the use of the house and furniture, it was entirely your own fault for agreeing to pay it, if you thought so, and very unnecessary to throw it in my face as you did on Tuesday. It will be none too much to make up for wear and tear of two families and three children, an arrangement I strongly disapprove of, and would never have agreed to for any consideration whatsoever.'

Effectively on notice to leave Millbrook as soon as possible, Bailey was now having to juggle his job and the replies to his ads as well as trying to find suitable new accommodation nearby where he could move his family, continue as a local milk roundsman and pursue the notation. Towards the end of August, he spotted an advertisement in the *Bucks Free Press* describing a Barn Cottage available to let in Church Road, Little Marlow, at 30 shillings a week, furnished throughout, complete with piano.

The ad had been placed in the paper by Miss Alice Boney on behalf of her mother, Charlotte Boney, with whom she lived in Hove, Brighton. Mrs Boney had bought the cottage in 1917 for £410 when it was one of the tied properties being sold off that year by the Bradish-Ellames family, owners of the village's Manor House and much surrounding land and housing.

Curiously, the name 'Barn Cottage' doesn't actually figure in the official cottage deeds, which make reference instead to 'The Old Bakery'. That was, for years, the prime use of the building up until around 1915. The name, referring to the large barn that ran east to west along the north side of the property, seems more likely to have been unofficially adopted for general use by both the new owner and, subsequently, in the press coverage of the case.

It was certainly in this guise that the *Maidenhead Advertiser*, which regularly covered Little Marlow district news, offered around the time of the crime the following, and extremely alluring, description of the property, more worthy of an estate agent's blurb than a résumé for the site of a slaying:

> *A more artistic, rustic cottage could not be imagined – old, plainly built and rambling, but a veritable picture for a country house. The main part, with gabled roof, clothed in Virginia creeper, the living portion forming the second section, the quaint bent window, the rustic lintel and door-posts with a horseshoe nailed to the door, the barn with the high roof standing next to the living portion, and from which the cottage takes its name, form as a group a most handsome rural residence. It has of late been owned by some ladies [sic], who let it for the summer season, and it is stylishly furnished. There is said to be eleven rooms, but beyond the hall and the chief rooms downstairs, the rest are small rooms. There is a garden on the north side with fruit trees, wire-baskets, water butt, and other country accessories. In the front is an old-fashioned garden, with just one solitary rose on the solitary rose bush. In every way a luxurious little country 'nest'. It had been occupied by summer visitors all the season.*

The paper then went on to speculate mischievously as to how a man of Bailey's means could afford such a place.

In the meantime, on 16 September, Bailey had met up with Miss Boney and she showed him round the place. She let him play the piano and he remarked that it needed tuning. She agreed and suggested he arrange it. He and his family moved in the next day.

A week later, Bailey jotted a letter to her explaining he'd contacted a piano tuner who'd done his stuff successfully – and would be sending her an account. He then wrote, 'I should like to ask you whether you are disposed to sell this property as it is. I should be willing to pay £550 as it is at present. Can also put you on to a good thing in my possession …' (was Bailey trying to interest her in his musical system?) '… but I want no bother through agents. I should esteem a reply, but I shall be engaged until the end of the week ending 9th of October, if you would like an interview. I am faithfully yours, GA Bailey.'

Bailey's obvious pleasure in Barn Cottage and its future possibilities contrasted rather sharply with an acrimonious end to his let of Millbrook. A few days before he made his offer to buy, he received a letter from Miss Hillary complaining that his final rent payment was 10s short and that if he didn't pay up 'within a few days' she would place the matter in the hands of a solicitor 'and claim another week's rent in lieu of notice, as you had no right to leave the house in the way you did without letting me know in time to take it over when you left. Please return broken wire mat missing from coal shed, which I saw at the door when I called to see you on Saturday.'

His immediate reply was short and slightly sinister: 'Miss M Hillary, I should advise you not to try bluff, it may lead to unpleasant consequences to yourself. P.S. On receipt of name and address of your solicitor I shall be only too pleased to hand them on to firm acting for me.'

On or around the time Bailey moved into Barn Cottage, he began increasingly to take time off from his milk round because of illness. Kate went to the dairy in Bourne End on 27 September to pick up her husband's wage packet.

That same day, Edwin Hall received the following letter from Bailey:

> *I have been impressed by your generosity re paying me a full week's money while I have been on the sick list, a thing I did not expect, or would not have asked for it, but at the same time I have come to work when I should not have done so, because I understood how you were placed with Mr Thorne* [another roundsman] *away. It is unfortunate, but unavoidable, and the first time I have been compelled to give in. I have visited the doctor again this afternoon, and it is at my own risk that I come to work until the plasters are off (lungs). It goes against the grain for me to lay up idle, also it is useless for me to come one day and lay up the next, aggravating the malady, which with short and proper treatment will enable me to resume work in a proper manner, also a satisfactory manner, which has been far from the case from my point of view on the few days that I have turned up, and hardly able to grasp what I am doing.*

Four days later, Mr Hall received a further letter from Bailey, dated 29 September: 'I shall be prepared to take up duties on Saturday [2 October]. Your obedient servant, GA Bailey.' He never returned.

On the day Bailey wrote his second letter to Mr Hall, two of his pupils, Miss Edwards and Miss Field, arrived at Barn Cottage around 10.30am, followed soon after by Miss Marks, and they all worked together on the musical notation. The session finished at 12.30pm when Miss Marks was told she was to stay the night and to be relieved the next day by Miss Edwards and Miss Field. Miss Marks, who had given up a 30-bob-a-week job in a grocery shop to work on the notation, was then given 4s for lunch and told by Bailey to return at 7.00pm. During the afternoon, Eliza Hester and Helen Hester, who lived next door at the Post Office-cum-village stores, separately saw and spoke to Kate who seemed happy and cheerful. They never saw either her or Hollie again after that.

What actually, or allegedly, then occurred at Barn Cottage between the final sighting of Kate sometime before 4.00pm on Wednesday, 29 September and the discovery of her body three days later would begin properly to unfold later in evidence at the various hearings. What is beyond dispute is that, the following morning, after Miss Marks left the property, having, she would subsequently claim, endured a night of terror, Bailey was visited by a local clergyman, Reverend Allen, to whom she had complained that morning about the milkman's conduct.

The same complaint soon reached the ears of Inspector William West, based at Marlow, who immediately contacted Supt George Kirby at High Wycombe. As a result, Supt Kirby then spoke to Miss Marks' father, Reuben, about his daughter's allegations. The next morning, 1 October, Inspector West decided to visit Barn Cottage under his own steam but found the place 'all shut up'. He contacted Supt Kirby again and they agreed to meet up the next day in Little Marlow to see if the matter needed to be taken further. At around 9.00am, they banged on the front door, which seemed to be fastened from the inside, but got no response. Several windows were, however, open and the two police officers managed to climb into the house through one of them.

The ground floor consisted, principally, of the hall, a sitting room, the old bakery area, kitchen and parlour, or dining room, in which they discovered tea laid out on the table – a plate of bread and butter, some cake, buns, two dishes of jam and what looked, they thought, like a milk pudding. There was nothing downstairs to arouse their suspicions any further. So they decided to go upstairs and take a closer look at the bedrooms.

Two of the four bedrooms led directly off the landing. In the first bedroom, on the right of the landing at the top of the stairs, they found some men's clothing lying on the floor. In the next bedroom, on the left of the stairs, the bedclothes were much disarranged. They then passed through the third – the 'master' bedroom, which overlooked the road outside and the cricket field opposite – which was only accessible via a door in the second room; then, finally, into the fourth, a back bedroom, which led off the main room.

There, they saw two single bedsteads – one, a camp bed neatly covered over with a counterpane. They pulled it back and, underneath the bed, wrapped in a sheet, was a body, which they immediately assumed to be Kate. She was lying on her back with her head facing towards a window that looked out on the yard at the back of the cottage. Surmising that she'd been dead for a while, several hours at least, the officers covered her face and left the house before stopping off, first, to have a quick word next door with Mr Hester who ran the Post Office and village stores.

While Supt Kirby began urgently to get 'enquiries' under way, Inspector West went to Marlow to try to find a doctor who could come as quickly as possible to examine the corpse. As luck would have it, he spotted one of the town's GPs, Dr Francis Wills, in the High Street deep in conversation with another local medic, Dr Dunbar Dickson. They agreed to go together immediately to Barn Cottage.

Their preliminary examination indicated that the body was of a woman 'about 25 years in age; rigor mortis has set in, more in the legs than the arms; her face was discoloured, a blue purplish colour; around the mouth there was a red-stained mucous which also covered the right eye cavity'. The neck was turning to green over the shoulder blade; the right hand was clenched and the left hand was outstretched. They removed Kate's clothing and found that her breasts were well developed and abdomen well extended. When they turned the body over, her back was stained red and a red corrosive liquid issued from her mouth. There were, however, no obvious marks of violence, such as bruises or scratches, nothing outwardly to account for death. However, Dr Wills did (although Dr Dickson would say later he didn't) detect an almond-like odour. In their opinion, she had been dead three to four days, and a proper post-mortem examination would be necessary.

Of Bailey and little Hollie, there was still no sign. Not for long, though. On Saturday evening, PC Henry Poole, from Marlow Police Station, was instructed by his superiors to go to Reading, where, at around 7.45pm, he met up at the railway station with Detective Sergeant Oliver Purdy of the Borough Police. Barely three-quarters-of-an-hour later, at 8.30pm, they spotted Bailey standing alone under a street lamp close to the railway station. The policemen approached him from behind before grabbing his arms. DS Purdy asked him if his name was Bailey, to which he replied, 'No.' He then asked him if he knew his Marlow colleague, to which Bailey also responded in the negative – which was odd since Bailey and Poole had talked in Marlow just a week earlier when Bailey was in town with Kate.

With that, they manhandled him to the police station, where he was searched. They found a bottle containing some prussic acid in his possession, and another containing opium as well as the copy of a telegram sent to Miss Field, requesting her to come to Barn Cottage on Sunday not Saturday 'as death had occurred', together with a letter addressed to the Coroner. Bailey also told them that Hollie was safe, staying with his sister and her husband in Swindon and that 'she must stay there; I do not want to see her again'. Purdy then told Bailey, who had been stripped and given a blanket to keep himself warm, that he was to be arrested for murder and would be kept at Reading until handed over to the Marlow Police.

The *Daily Mail* reported, triumphantly: 'The arrest was effected without the aid of Scotland Yard and it is said that use of motorcycles was responsible for the speedy capture.'

Shortly after Bailey was taken into custody, Inspector West arrived in Reading and explained to the prisoner how he and Supt Kirby had entered Barn Cottage earlier that day and found Kate, after which the doctors had been called in to examine her. 'It is now my duty,' he announced formally, 'to charge you with killing and murdering your wife on or about 29 September.' He asked the prisoner if he understood the charge against him to which Bailey answered, 'Yes.' He then officially cautioned Bailey, who replied calmly, 'I don't think I have anything to say. Let's get back to Marlow as quick as we can,' which they did, later that same night.

The following morning, on the Sunday, Inspector West and Supt Kirby met up again and made a further search of Barn Cottage. This time round, they unearthed quite a sizeable trawl of significant items. In a small wooden box, they discovered some bottles; among them one containing extract of ergot, a packet of perchlorate of mercury and an empty phial marked 'Devatol. Reg A'. In addition, there was an eggcup, a small glass, a tin of adhesive plaster and a packet of cotton wool. There were also two other small boxes, with bottles containing tincture of iodine, hydrogen peroxide and Freeman's chlorodyne; on another bottle of iodine was marked 'Poison, not to be taken'; then there was a packet of chloral hydrate and a small swab.

On the copper (a large kitchen utensil) they found a tin of sulphur, a packet of Glauber's salts (used as a laxative), a box of zinc ointment and a tin box containing packets of aloes and senna. There was a piece of paper, the draft of an order to the chemist, on which was written the names of various drugs. In the kitchen and on the dresser they found a bottle containing a pink fluid of what looked like lemonade. In the coal scuttle was part of a book relating to instructions for the use of Devatol.

In a bureau were a number of letters from applicants to Bailey's newspaper ads including one from Miss Tubb, which had scrawled at the bottom in Bailey's handwriting, 'a very good figure'. They also found some sealing wax, which seemed to correspond with that used on the top of a bottle of prussic acid, and three letters from the Prudential Assurance Company, each dated 11 September, and addressed to Bailey, Kate and Hollie, pointing out that the premiums hadn't been paid since February.

That afternoon, soon after 3.00pm, Dr Bernard Spilsbury, the Home Office pathologist, arrived in Little Marlow to conduct his official post-mortem, assisted by Dr Wills. Externally, he found Kate well nourished, the abdomen was as previously described, and decomposition was advancing. The pupils of the eyes were slightly dilated and the whites of the eyes were congested; a reddish fluid had escaped from the mouth and nostrils. Her hands were clenched, the fingernails were blue.

Internally, the brain and covering of the skull and scalp were, Dr Spilsbury noted, healthy and free from injury. On the surface of the brain there was congestion; there were tiny blood spots on the surface of the heart and lungs; the heart itself was flabby and slightly dilated; the muscles, arteries and valves were also healthy. There was no disease of any kind of the organs. The tongue was red and inflamed, and the back of the tongue and gullet were congested. The stomach contained some fluid, which had a putrid odour, and Dr Spilsbury, like Dr Wills earlier, thought he detected a faint odour suggesting prussic acid. He also confirmed the doctors' earlier verdict that Kate had been dead not less than three days.

Dr Spilsbury concluded that the victim was at least six months pregnant but there was no sign of any instrumental attempt to secure an abortion. Kate's death, he told the police, was consistent with prussic-acid poisoning.

Not long after he and Supt Kirby had completed their second, and more comprehensive, sweep of Barn Cottage, and probably around the time Drs Spilsbury and Wills were beginning to minutely examine Kate, Inspector West took a cup of tea into Bailey at the cells in Marlow.

'If I make a statement to you,' Bailey asked West, 'do you think you will be able to get my case settled at the next Assizes?' The prisoner hadn't yet seemed fully to have grasped the enormity of the charge against him, having learned that they were due to begin at Aylesbury in just ten days' time, from 13 October.

'If you wish to make a statement,' said West, 'you can do so; but it will not help you to get your case settled then.'

Deciding against making a statement in that case, Bailey asked instead when the inquest was likely to get under way because, he told West, firmly, 'I want to attend.'

So ended the first act of what would unfold as a classic three-act drama. Officially, it was now a case of wilful murder. Even in custody, Bailey would remain an active and ever more compelling player in an extraordinary saga whose surface had barely been scratched. For the accused man, it was just another tragic twist on what he would, euphemistically, describe as 'a simple story of love and devotion'.

2

SCENE OF THE CRIME

Until the tumultuous events of September, the only other crime that seems to have been worth reporting that year in Little Marlow was committed some months earlier when three local men were charged with stealing a chicken, worth 10s, from a farm in the north of the parish. One of the men, Jas Clark, was further charged with 'maliciously killing a fowl', one of two that a witness – Henry Field, son of Wood Barn Farm's owner, George Field – actually saw him shoot in a lane alongside the family property.

After the trio made off, Henry picked up some feathers, several wads of a cartridge and the dead chicken that had been left behind, all of which were later produced in evidence at Marlow Police Court. On the afternoon of the alleged poaching, the three defendants were picked up and taken to Marlow Police Station where they were asked to account for their movements earlier that day. Clark claimed to have been at a football match, while the two other prisoners, brothers Sidney and Harry Price, said they'd been for 'a walk round'. Their case wasn't helped by the fact that in Sidney's pocket they found feathers similar to the ones gathered earlier by Henry Field as well as six cartridges. In Court, Clark, who, despite having many previous convictions, continued to protest his innocence, was fined £5 and the other two men 10s each. According to a local newspaper report, 'the money was paid'.

At least they didn't suffer the same fate as three men elsewhere in the same county some 30 years earlier. On that occasion, Frederick Eggleton, Charles Rayner and Walter Smith – notorious poachers, all armed with guns – were confronted in the woods of a large estate at night by two zealous keepers carrying just clubs. In the resulting fracas, the keepers were both shot to death. At the end of a controversial trial where it was argued that the poachers were guilty merely of manslaughter because they were attempting to defend themselves, all three men were convicted; two, Eggleton and Rayner, were hanged for murder, while Smith received 20 years' penal servitude after his plea of manslaughter was accepted by the jury.

Before the arrival of George Arthur Bailey, that kind of violent sensation would have seemed anathema to a community like Little Marlow, described in a contemporary *Kelly's Directory* as 'a widely scattered place, with a few farms and shops, and bounded on the south by the Thames'. Although less than 30 miles from London, it was, in the days before mass cars and motorways, the heart of the country. Almost exactly halfway between the more populous towns of Marlow and Bourne End, Little Marlow was a 'particularly neat and select hamlet, the villas being mostly let out for the summer visitors', according to the *Maidenhead Advertiser* in October 1920. Its tiny village centre in an otherwise sprawling parish was still mourning the loss of some of its finest young men, most in their twenties, who'd either died in action during the Great War, or later succumbed to their injuries back home.

Men like Charles Werrell and William Napper, both aged 20, of the Oxford & Bucks Light Infantry. Werrell, who had been working in the gardens of the Manor House at the outbreak of war, managed to join up in June 1915 by 'making an addition to his age'. He was killed in France less than two months before the Armistice. Napper, who'd been educated at the village school and was employed by a local cycle-maker, died of his wounds in Belgium a year earlier. Percy Twitchen, from one of Little Marlow's oldest families – there are local records of Twitchens from 1767 – fought with the Hampshire Regiment and died in Palestine aged 26. Charles Harrowing was another Oxford & Bucks Light infantryman, a corporal, son of a groom, whose final resting place was Doiran Military Cemetery in Northern Greece. He was 25.

Philip Harris, one of six children, was a year younger when he died in action on 26 May 1915 and is 'remembered with honour' on the Le Touret Memorial at the Pas de Calais. The exception to this 20-something roll-call was Worcestershire-born William Tolman who, before enlisting, worked in the village as a domestic chauffeur, probably at the Manor House. He was 46 when badly injured serving with the Motor Ambulance Division of the Royal Army Service Corps and died at home just after New Year, 1916.

These are just a handful of names from among a longer list of the Little Marlow fallen that are inscribed on a memorial to the war dead of the wider parish affixed to a wall on the south aisle of the village's 12th-century church, St John the Baptist. On the first Sunday in July that year, during an afternoon service whose large congregation almost overflowed the church, that memorial, executed in statuary marble, locally designed and paid for by public subscription, was officially unveiled. The vicar, Rev John Best, read out the list of names, no fewer than 42 in all, or, more revealingly, around 4 per cent of the entire parish population.

So maybe it wasn't hugely surprising that, when, less than three months on, the spectre of violent death through the Bailey trial suddenly encroached again on a still grief-stricken community, the effect was seemingly seismic and the subsequent events followed in occasionally hysterical fashion with, according to local newspaper reports, 'booing and groans' regularly accompanying Bailey's arrivals and exits at the various hearings following his arrest.

The first of these was two days later when, at Marlow Police Court, in the briefest of proceedings, Bailey was charged with 'feloniously killing and murdering' Kate. He made no reply and was remanded to Oxford Prison. A large crowd had assembled outside and, as Bailey, together with two policemen, climbed into a car on his way to Oxford, his smile to the crowd was said to have turned to a flush as angry shouts rang out from women lining the pavement. Wearing a bowler hat, fawn raincoat and a stripy tie, he then covered his face with the hat until the car managed to drive off.

The following morning at 11.00am sharp, Arthur Charsley, the Coroner for South Bucks, opened the inquest into Kate's death. The venue was The King's Head, the bigger of the village's two pubs, 400 years old with curved walls, beamed ceilings and less than 150 yards from Barn Cottage.

In attendance was an all-male jury of 12 Marlow residents of whom Mr AE Barnard was selected to be foreman. The two senior officers in the case – Supt Kirby and Inspector West – along with PC Gray represented the police, Gray doubling up as Coroner's Officer. Kirby and West offered brief accounts of the discovery and condition of the body and that 'a man named George Arthur Bailey was in custody', while Bailey's brother-in-law, James Jennings, confirmed that the body was indeed that of his sister-in-law, adding, during the briefest of questioning, that the couple had always seemed to have been on 'affectionate terms' and that he knew of no reason why Bailey should have wanted to murder Kate. Bailey's mother, Betsy, who had travelled more than 200 miles from her home at Berrynarbor in North Devon, was not required to give evidence.

Mr Charsley brought the inquest to a close, explaining that sufficient evidence had been given for him to grant an order for burial. He told the Court that he would in due course reconvene the proceedings at Marlow Police Court to make it more convenient for the jury. Examination of Kate's stomach contents by Dr Spilsbury, the Home Office pathologist, would, he added, probably be completed in about three weeks' time.

The next afternoon, a tiny congregation mainly comprising old Mrs Bailey, James Jennings and George Weston, a local official who'd made the arrangements, attended Kate's funeral at St John the Baptist, conducted by Rev Best. Later that afternoon, as the light was fading fast, Kate was buried, not in the churchyard but at the cemetery about half a mile away off Fern Lane. Her final resting place, known as Plot 256, was as anonymous as most of her short, sad life.

Less than a week later, shortly before midday on 12 October, Bailey, his black hair tinged with grey and now sporting several days' growth, was wearing the same fawn coat and bowler hat when he made a second, even shorter appearance at Marlow Police Court; again he was remanded in custody after the traditional request by Supt Kirby. The prisoner bowed towards the Magistrate, Mr Buckingham, and visibly mouthed 'Thank you' before being hurried out of the dock.

His journey to Marlow wasn't, however, without incident. Changing trains at Bourne End for the branch line, known as 'The Marlow Donkey', the ever-smiling Bailey was greeted by a hostile crowd, again mostly women, who booed him roundly. Outside Marlow Station, just a stop away, an even larger crowd had gathered, which, like the throng around the Police Court as he climbed out of a taxi, made its aggressive feelings loudly heard. 'Even this did not disconcert him,' reported the *Bucks Free Press*, 'and once again there was a cynical smile on his countenance.'

The return journey was no less fraught, with angry women this time actually spilling on to the platform itself at Marlow. As cameras representing local and national newspapers flashed, Bailey spotted one in particular and shouted, 'All right, old boy,' as he tried, unsuccessfully, to shield his face. He was quickly bundled into the train and the blinds of the carriage window were drawn down.

In an attempt to instil a little more colour into its report of the day's short but dramatic proceedings, the *Bucks Free Press* included an interview with an unnamed 'lady resident of Bourne End' who told the paper that Bailey was very much liked in the district by his milk-round customers. 'He was always speaking about his dear wife (the deceased woman) and was loud in his praise of her capabilities. I remember him telling me that he was run down, and was going to have a week's rest. I expressed the hope that he would benefit by the change. He wished me "Good day!" and left my door. It was during his week's rest and change that his poor wife was found dead.'

Another week, and yet another two-minute appearance as Bailey underwent, on 21 October, his third Oxford round trip, this time before a full strength of Marlow Magistrates and with Supt Kirby advising the Court that, following another seven days' remand, the prisoner's next appearance might require at least two days at Marlow with overnight stays for the accused. The brevity of the visit in no way lessened the continuing ill will, with 'shrieking and hissing' now added to the familiar booing of the accused. The numbers striving to access the Court would have filled the place half a dozen times over. The crush getting in provided 'a spectacle that was unbecoming'. Meanwhile, there was still no news of a resumed inquest.

This almost frenzied local antagonism was rather neatly mirrored in another, much higher-profile case of alleged wife poisoning, which happened to coincide almost exactly with these opening salvoes against Bailey. In west Wales, 45-year-old solicitor Harold Greenwood was on trial for killing his wife Mabel, whose death in June 1919 was originally attributed to heart disease. After the funeral, rumours began in the Greenwoods' home town of Kidwelly that her death had been far from natural, a buzz exacerbated by Greenwood remarrying just four months after Mabel's demise.

In April 1920, her body was exhumed and the subsequent inquest recorded that she had died from acute arsenic poisoning, which had been administered by her husband. On hearing this verdict, the public present apparently broke into rapturous applause. In the event, Greenwood would, following a very skilful defence by the greatest criminal lawyer of his day, Sir Edward Marshall Hall, be acquitted, although he died a broken man just nine years later.

The 'phoney war' of the preliminary hearings finally gave way to the tooth-and-claw of a full-scale, pre-trial inquiry into the case against Bailey which, from its outset on 28 October, prompted garish local headlines like 'SENSATIONAL EVIDENCE', 'PRISONER'S DRAMATIC OUTBURST' and 'LARGE CROWDS BESIEGE THE COURT HOUSE'.

According to FJ Sims, the Assistant Public Prosecutor, the story given to the Magistrates would be 'one of the most remarkable ever heard in a Court of Justice'. The first 'sensation' came quite early on the first day of a three-day hearing, with the introduction of a letter that had been discovered soon after Bailey's arrest 'addressed to the Coroner via the Police'. This would be the first of a number of strange, rambling, seemingly suicidal yet oddly compelling documents composed by Bailey that would come under the public gaze over the next few months. It read:

Please do not worry my people. There is no need to divulge where I come from, or divulge that I belong to so and so. For my dead mother's [very odd this for, as we will discover, his mother is actually very much alive if not terribly well] *and brothers' and sisters' sake. There is no need to call any witnesses for evidence. This is the first act* [Bailey pointed out on Day Two that this should have read 'the final act' but had been copied out wrongly] *of an unbalanced yet vigorous brain. My darling is waiting for me. I gave her hers first; then I follow, the same death that she died. I handed the poison to her, she believed my statements. They are our secret. I pray God that he lets us be united as we have always believed we should be. She is asking for me. For her child now. I have contemplated horrible things — almost accomplished them. Please take great care of the music I leave behind. It is the notation of the future. If the old school would only overcome their jealousy, their conservatism and prejudice. I have shown several young ladies its simplicity. Miss Field, Miss Edwards, Miss Marks can explain more.*

I heard my darling die on Wednesday 29th Sept, 7.15pm. I have waited my fate and now I meet it. My own dear wife knows and knew but she is so brave, so staunch. Please that God will forgive her. Forgive me. Please do not let this tragedy destroy the future of this notation but that someone with foresight will take it up. I ask no pardon from the world. I have ever been a source of worry and trouble. It has been harder to fight than I can resist and I have tried. But I know and knew that it must all end in some such way.

I should like our three bodies laid together. That is why I came back to take one last look. Give one last kiss to my beloved. I gave her stramonia first, then hydrocyanic. No blame attaches to the chemist. I always could bluff to attain my ends. Goodbye poor dear mother and my own dear sister Nellie and brother-in-law Jim. Wayward when young but easily to be corrected, if they had only known. I believe I have been broken-hearted since poor dad died and I failed to make good, but my own beloved wife Kitty understood me and loved me so much and I, yes in my own way my life has been given to her, no matter what I intended to do. It was always decided to go together and not to leave our baby behind. Please God, Father of all nature, forgive us all. But I do not believe in thy existence — as more simple than the Bible? Is tonight just our father who must recognise him as such.

My darling I am coming [written upside down]

The new music upstairs that will be found with our belongings is the system of the future. That this tragedy has followed within so short a period.

Wearing his perma-smile and now allowed to sit in the dock while taking copious notes, Bailey was charged not only with capital murder but also with a serious sexual offence against Miss Marks, one of the three above-mentioned young women who had answered his newspaper ads. Without legal representation at this stage, he also occasionally asked questions of the various witnesses, mostly to try to establish that he and Kate had been on very happy terms. However, in the case of Miss Marks who, under Mr Sims' careful probing, gave a very full and distressing account of her night at Barn Cottage while Kate lay dead in the next room, Bailey restricted himself to just one question: 'You allege that these serious happenings occurred?' To which she replied simply, 'Yes.'

Since most of the same witnesses' testimony before the Magistrates and, later, the inquest will be more carefully examined in due course when it comes to the actual coverage of Bailey's trial, here it is perhaps sufficient occasionally to note some of the prisoner's own cross-examination of them in the course of the two hearings. The latter was strung out because of adjournments across two months, before Bailey would later get the benefit of Counsel at the Assizes.

Mr Sims was just about to get Day Two under way by calling more witnesses when Bailey – who seemed to have acquired an appetite for advocacy on Day One –

stepped in with: 'I am sorry, your Worships, to interrupt the proceedings of the Court, but I would like to ask you to grant me legal aid ...' to which Mr Shone, the Magistrates' Clerk, replied, 'The Court has no power to grant a certificate of legal aid; they can only do so when the nature of the defence is disclosed.'

The Chairman, Mr Morgan, added, 'We must refuse it. You can make your application when you are before a Judge, if you are committed for trial.'

Bailey retorted, 'I have several witnesses to call. Then their evidence will be placed on the depositions.'

Mr Morgan reassured him, 'You shall have every opportunity to call whom you wish.'

The revelation of the Coroner's letter the previous day was almost matched this morning by the disclosure of another of Bailey's colourful statements, this time given verbally and, according to PC John Gray who was in charge of the prisoner at Marlow Police Station after his arrest, entirely unsolicited. Reading from his notes, PC Gray told the Court that Bailey had confided to him:

'Between me and you, me and Kit [Kate] were in the garden on Wednesday evening, and then almost 5.00pm we went indoors and had tea, some buns and bread and butter. Her last words to me were, "You will have to come, too." We were very loving to one another. I had already made up my mind what to do; but although I am an atheist, it came across my mind that we should be parted for ever. On Thursday evening, I locked the front door, took the child, and put the key through the letterbox and went off. My intentions were to come back to Little Marlow on

Saturday. I done wrong in telling them at Swindon that my wife was at Wycombe Hospital. It has made it look black against me. I should have made a clear statement to Inspector West, but as it will not help the Court proceedings, I shall keep quiet. If this goes against me, I wish all my things at Barn Cottage shall be burnt, except the push chair, and I want that to be given to my little girl.'

'If I remember rightly, about "her last words",' Bailey asked PC Gray, 'I think I stated "We were often talking about these things"?'

'No,' replied the police officer confidently.

'You had a lot to remember; perhaps you cannot recollect,' Bailey noted, with a hint of sarcasm worthy of a more experienced advocate.

He also took his brother-in-law to task after Jim Jennings told Mr Sims that Bailey had 'a dirty smile' on his face when he told him and his sister Helen that he'd be returning to Little Marlow after reporting that Kate had died.

'You said that I had a "dirty smile" on my face? Give us a clearer explanation of what you mean?'

'It was not a clear smile.'

'Malicious or evil?'

'I could not say that.'

Then followed the curious sight of brother cross-examining sister as Bailey questioned Helen Jennings on the matter of his music.

'We used to come to you in all our troubles and trials?'

'Yes, you did.'

'Was I not agitated about a system of music that had been published and did I not write off for a copy?'

'Yes.'

'Did I not mention to you that my ideas had been stolen?'

'You did.'

'I sent off for a copy, and when I received it, did I not say, "Thank God, it is not mine"?'

'Yes.'

'And was I not much relieved?'

'Yes.'

The *Bucks Free Press* noted that Bailey was 'moved to tears' for the first time while Helen was giving evidence. It also observed that Bailey's mother was present in Court, cutting 'a pathetic figure, her face buried in her hands'.

The matter of the accused's music came into much sharper focus with the evidence of Marlow-based musicologist Dr Samuel Bath; not in a good way, though. He said he had examined examples of the notation as shown by two of Bailey's 'students', Miss Marks and Miss Field, and found them to be 'grossly grotesque'. To much laughter from the Court, he likened one of them to 'a crude drawing of a trail of tadpoles seeking an incubator'. He added that he thought its value was nil and anyone trying to learn it, if they could, which he doubted, would be no better off.

After this, Bailey was naturally anxious for some kind of comeback.

'Do you understand that it is a new staff system?'

'I do not admit it is a new system.'

'Have you had no opportunity of being initiated into the simplicity of this new system?'

'No.'

'That is all I have to ask,' concluded Bailey, probably realising he was on a hiding to nothing with Dr Bath.

But it didn't quite end there, with Mr Sims asking the witness, 'Would you be able to play this system on the piano?'

'No. I should hardly know which way to begin it,' Dr Bath replied unswervingly, provoking more gales of laughter.

This time, Bailey's retort smacked of desperation. 'There are other scripts in the possession of the police that explain this system of music.'

The prisoner's lot took another unhappy turn straight after Dr Bath had given evidence with the arrival next in the witness box of one William Geo Day, described as a 'valet of 14, Princes Gardens, London'. Day, who said his home was in Bourne End where he was living with his mother at the time, told the Court that on 15 September he'd been riding his bike back from Marlow during the evening and encountered Bailey and his wife about 50 yards from Barn Cottage. He alleged that he saw the prisoner with his right arm around Kate's throat and left arm about her waist, and that he heard Bailey tell her, 'My God, I will put an end to you.' He cycled on and the next day returned to London where, a little over a fortnight later, after being prompted by the butler, he saw pictures of Bailey in the *Daily Mirror* and the *Daily Graphic*. At that, he got in touch straight away with Supt Kirby and with his local police in Chelsea.

'Whereabouts did this alleged episode take place?' Bailey asked Day.

'About 30 yards down the lane.'

'Was it in an open field?'

'No … on the roadway.'

'How was she dressed?'

'I have an idea she was dressed in a check costume.'

'I have no more questions to ask, your Worships.'

Following this unsatisfactory exchange – for Bailey, at least – Mr Sims asked for a further remand until the following

Monday when he would call all the various medical witnesses. Mr Morgan told Bailey that he should prepare his own list of witnesses giving an idea of their evidence so the Magistrates could then decide whether it was relevant or not. Before being taken back to Oxford, Bailey said that he hoped the police could be influenced to allow him a clean collar and shirt as well as a decent shave before the resumption after the weekend.

When he reappeared 48 hours later in the dock at Marlow, it was obvious from his still somewhat dishevelled appearance that he hadn't been granted any of the above. The medical experts, including the Home Office pathologist, Dr Bernard Spilsbury, and official analyst John Webster, who only weeks earlier had been together on duty at the Kidwelly case in Carmarthen, duly gave their evidence. At its conclusion, Mr Sims told the Court that that was the case for the Prosecution. Then the Chairman explained to Bailey that he was now allowed to give evidence and call witnesses, in that specific order.

Bailey stood up in the dock and said:

'Your Worships, I beg to emphatically deny both charges laid against me. I hope to prove that my purpose in obtaining these various drugs and sundries was for the purpose of taking up farrier work – not as a qualified veterinary surgeon – for the purpose of raising money. That the cyanide of potassium was ordered for the purposes stated to Miss Parsons [a photographer's assistant with whom the Baileys had shared accommodation at Millbrook and from whom George had hoped to obtain poison in order, he claimed, to destroy wasps' nests]. I hope to prove that my system of staff notation is all that I claim for it, and not a grotesque absurdity; that it was not a farce, or a cloak for nefarious designs, but the fruits of hard study and investigation. That I did not commit a felonious assault or attempted rape on the person of Miss Marks. That I did not threaten to assault my wife at Little Marlow; we were not there; that evidence is utterly false. That in the main, the evidence of the Prosecution is built up on unreliable facts and supposition. That I acted and thought throughout the whole period, from my coming to Millbrook, to the taking of and the living at Barn Cottage in an abnormal [sic] manner, under great stress of mind, I agree. That this remarkable case is just a simple story of love and devotion on both sides; hardships; trials surmounted; triumph within sight; then disaster and collapse. So I reserve my defence and desire to plead legal aid to assist me in my defence.'

The Chairman told Bailey that he would be committed for trial at the Bucks Assizes on both the capital charge and for attempted indecent assault. However, Mr Morgan added, 'We cannot grant you a certificate for legal aid, but Mr Shone [the Clerk] will send all particulars of your case to the Home Secretary.' He then congratulated the police for their efforts, noting Supt Kirby and Inspector West, 'who had very slender evidence on which to work, and which resulted in a very clever arrest of the accused man'.

The following day, many of the same faces, including Bailey who'd asked to attend, were reassembled back at Marlow Police Court for a resumption of the much-adjourned inquest. They also numbered among them the London-based valet Mr Day who had, on Day Two before the Magistrates, delivered his bombshell suggesting that a fortnight before Kate died, he'd actually witnessed physical and verbal violence involving the prisoner and his late wife. He repeated his assertion before the Coroner and jury.

One of the jury asked him, 'Did you not interfere when the man made that remark?'

'Not at all ... simply a case of man and wife.'

'And you did not inform the police?'

'No.'

Bailey asked, 'In which direction was my wife's face?'

'Marlow.'

'At 9.30 at night, you recognised us on a dark night?'

'It was not dark.' [It was in fact summertime.]

'What clothes was my wife wearing?'

'A plaid dress.'

'You said the other day she was wearing a check?'

'I wish to withdraw that word and substitute "plaid".'

'A very good witness.'

'I have since picked out the clothes from others shown me, and those produced are what Mrs Bailey was wearing on the evening in question.'

'At 9.30 on a dark night you say you recognised us?'

'Yes.'

'How tall was my wife?'

'I should say 5ft 6in or 5ft 7in.'

'Would you be surprised to learn that her height was 4ft 11in to 5ft?'

'I will not pledge myself as to the height.'

Much of the day's other evidence was simply a reprise of what had been heard before in another Court. However, shortly before the inquest was again adjourned, hopefully to resume the following Tuesday, Bailey's cross-examination featured once more after PC Poole and DS Purdy had furnished official details of Bailey's arrest in Reading.

'What state of mind did I appear to be in when you arrested me?'

'You appeared to be dazed at the time.'

'And yet I kept on making gruesome jokes?' [There is, sadly, no record of what these 'gruesome jokes' might have been.]

'Yes.'

In the event, all involved would have to endure yet another delay — it seems Mr Webster, the Home Office analyst, was caught up in a case at Maidstone, so the Coroner announced that, availability of experts permitting, the inquest would now be finally sorted on 26 November.

On this particular Friday, Bailey's arrival at Marlow was, for a change, almost low-key with the crowd, unaware of when he was actually due, smaller and less vociferous than before. Onlookers would, though, have noticed a change in his physical presence with now, the *Bucks Free Press* reported, 'streaks of grey in his otherwise black hair being very pronounced'.

Dr Spilsbury confirmed that death was due to poisoning by prussic acid and would have occurred any time between five minutes and half an hour of its administration.

After the various doctors had completed their evidence, Supt Kirby returned to the witness box and gave details of a discovery he and Inspector West had made during a comprehensive search of the bedrooms three days after Kate's body had been discovered. In a chest of drawers, they'd found a small box in which, among a number of photos and picture postcards, was a small book in which was written what appeared to be a letter that was neither dated nor signed. It opened: 'Mother, will you take care of little Hollie for me, or see she is taken care of: I can't stand it any longer …' and rambled a little in a rather self-pitying way about how difficult things were to bear. It ended with: 'God knows I have had it all taken out of me: the shame, the disgrace of it all … I can't always forget, if George can.'

After Mr Charsley finished reading out what seemed to be just the latest in a series of incendiary documents revealed during the course of the various pre-trial hearings, he asked Supt Kirby if he knew in whose handwriting was this distressing note.

'No, sir,' replied the doughty senior police officer from High Wycombe.

The Coroner then addressed the jury, summarising the case against Bailey and reminding them of some of Bailey's letters and statements including an exchange with PC Poole after he'd been taken to Reading Police Station following his arrest. 'Do not say anything to the people at Swindon about this. Between you and I, I might have had something else inside me, but you were a bit too fly for me.' When PC Poole later gave Bailey a blanket, the prisoner had remarked, 'I suppose I shall be colder later on.'

Mr Charsley told the jury that they must consider three questions: did Kate die from prussic acid or hydrocyanic acid poisoning? Was that poison administered to her, taken voluntarily by her, or was it taken by accident? And if they thought it was given to her, would they say who gave it to her? If the accused gave her the poison, then he must be found guilty of wilful murder.

Before the Court was cleared for the jury to consider their verdict, Bailey protested about Day's evidence, especially its inconsistency. The Coroner ruled that the jury could discard the evidence of Day from their minds, to which several of them piped up, 'We have already decided to do that.'

Mr Charsley asked the prisoner if he had anything further to say. 'No,' he replied, 'Mr RS Wood of High Wycombe and Thame is undertaking my defence,' referring to the senior partner in a firm of highly respected local solicitors.

It took the jury just 15 minutes to conclude that Kate was poisoned and that Bailey was responsible. The Coroner intoned the inevitable: 'George Arthur Bailey, it is my duty to commit you to the next Bucks Assizes on the charge of wilfully murdering your wife.'

The prisoner bowed, smiled – yes, that smile – and left the dock followed by a pair of warders. Before leaving Court for the return journey to Oxford Prison, Bailey called out to the representative of the *Bucks Free Press*, saying, 'If I do not see you at the Bucks Assizes, will you please see my sister and ask her what took place on the Tuesday before my wife died?'

'Do you mean Mrs Jennings?' came the reply.

'Yes,' said Bailey, 'You ask her … it will astound you.'

And with that, the legal preliminaries in the case of R v Bailey were finally completed ahead of the trial at Aylesbury which was likely to be quite soon after the turn of a new year. In less than two months, it wouldn't only be Bailey who would be facing an ordeal but also several of the young women who had fatefully answered his advertisements and would have to give evidence in a much wider glare of publicity.

For three older women from the Aylesbury area, however, there would be a different kind of test altogether at the Bucks Assizes, one that would make legal history.

Meanwhile, the local paper reported that, having completed all their analysis, the police had handed back Barn Cottage to the owner Mrs Boney and that it had been re-let.

3

LADIES AND GENTLEMEN
OF THE JURY

In a letter to the Editor of the *Times* dated 19 September 1919, and headlined 'LOCKING UP JURIES – AN INCONVENIENT PRACTICE', one Harry B Poland noted that 'the inconvenience to the jury is on some occasions very serious indeed. As soon as it is known that the case must last more than one day, the jurymen who have been sworn to try the case have to send to their homes for their necessary apparel. In Palmer's case, the trial lasted 12 days and the Staunton case 10 days so that juries were locked up over a Sunday. Consider what this means to many of the jurymen.'

Then Poland – actually the venerable Sir Harry Bodkin Poland KC, a veteran of 72 years at the bar and author of many a distinguished legal tome, including the lip-smackingly titled *Criminal Appeal Bill (1906) Examined* – opined, 'Suppose the Lord Chancellor's Bill to qualify women as jurors passes

Parliament, and suppose a case of murder is tried by six men and six women, they cannot very well be locked up together for the night; so a male bailiff will be wanted to look after the men and a female bailiff to look after the women, or perhaps only one woman.'

A knotty problem indeed, as outlined by Sir Harry, then aged 90, a former Recorder of Dover. He was succeeded in his post by his nephew, the even more distinguished Sir Archibald Bodkin KCB, a prosecutor in the Roger Casement treason trial and 'Brides in the Bath' murder case before becoming, in 1920, Director of Public Prosecutions. In that office for ten years, he became the scourge, in particular, of 'filth and obscenity' in literature. Particularly obsessed with lesbianism in literature – 'those wicked women, as I deem them' – he successfully launched a crusade against a well-known 'lesbian' trailblazer at the time, Radclyffe Hall's *The Well of Loneliness*, which was successfully prosecuted in 1928 and, as a result, remained generally unavailable in the UK for another 20 years.

Uncle Harry's own distaff concerns, meanwhile, were compounded just three months after his heartfelt *Times* missive with the Royal Assent, on 23 December 1919, of the Sex Disqualification (Removal) Act. This followed the passing a year earlier of the Representation of the People Act, which had granted women a limited right to vote after a long and sometimes violent struggle for suffrage. Section 1 of the subsequent 1919 Act stated in a typically pedantic, albeit ground-breaking, way: 'A person shall not be disqualified by sex or marriage from the exercise of any public function or from being appointed to or holding any civil or judicial office or post, or from entering or assuming or carrying on any civil profession or vocation, or for admission to any incorporated society (whether incorporated by Royal Charter or otherwise), [and a person shall not be exempted by sex or marriage from the liability to serve as a juror].'

Six months later, in a short report dated 28 July 1920, the *New York Times* screamed: 'FIRST WOMEN APPEAR ON JURY IN ENGLAND' with the intriguing strap-line, 'Sit Through Six Cases, Then Two Asked to be Excused to Attend to Home Duties'. The story, filed by the *Associated Press*, noted: 'The prosecuting Counsel in addressing the jury departed from the time worn "Gentlemen of the jury", and said, "Ladies and gentlemen of the jury". The new phrase caused a murmur throughout the court. The Counsel congratulated the women jurors for "at last taking their proper place in the administration of justice in England". He added that the cause of justice also was to be congratulated.'

The Counsel in question was Mr RE Dummett and the venue for this historic legal 'first' was Bristol Quarter Sessions. There, the jury heard the case against William Henry Ayton, 52, a dock labourer, for stealing parcels at Weston-super-Mare Station. It consisted of six men and six women, the latter drawn from a pool including at least three milliners, a draper, tobacconist and hat manufacturer.

In its report of the trial, the *Daily Mail*, before dealing with the actual proceedings, helpfully reminded its readers about the actual prerequisites for being a woman juror. She 'must be between the ages of 21 and 65, a householder assessed (in the provinces) at not less than £20 a year, the occupier of a house with not less than 15 windows, and a natural-born subject or an alien of not less than ten years' domicile.' Or, as the *Times* would put it, rather more succinctly, 'drawn from the middle classes'.

The enormity of the occasion, however, didn't stop two of

the selected women jurors at the start of proceedings from expressing some initial concern about their pioneering duties to the Recorder, Dr W Blake Odgers KC. One told him she was concerned about her children whom she had had to leave at home, while another explained she had had to close her shop while she was in Court. Those comments duly noted, after which Mr Dummett then opened the case for the Prosecution against Ayton with: 'Ladies and gentlemen of the jury – this is the first occasion on which I have used this unfamiliar phrase. As far as I know, it has not been used before in the annals of the jurisdiction in this country, certainly not in this city …' Ayton, who, the Court was told, 'had given way to drink, for which he had a weakness', was duly found guilty and sentenced to 12 months' imprisonment.

On this momentous day, the evenly mixed jury also heard cases against a 31-year-old riveter accused of indecently assaulting two girls at Clifton, a teenager charged with breaking and entering and stealing (including three cigarettes), and a man aged 33 accused of stealing a motorbike. At the end of the sitting, some of the women asked to be excused from further duties 'on account of domestic and business ties'. Their request was granted.

Others, however, volunteered to stay on during the whole session. At the end of its report, the *Daily Mail*, beneath the strapline 'Census of Women Jurors', revealed that 'assistant overseers throughout the kingdom have received instructions to prepare by September a list of men and women competent to sit on juries. "It's been difficult enough to get women on the voters' lists, but it will be more difficult to get their ages for a jury list," said an assistant overseer yesterday.'

Where Bristol led, so the Central Criminal Court at the Old Bailey would follow, one might suggest belatedly, half a year later when, at its January Sessions, no fewer than 50 women were summoned – apparently, the majority from Hampstead – to serve. Their empanelling took place, as was the custom, in the Court of the Common Serjeant – the Old Bailey's second most senior permanent Judge. He was none other than Henry (later Sir Henry) Fielding Dickens KC, eighth of ten children to Charles Dickens, then in the fourth of 15 years in that prestigious law office.

In a scene that would have been worthy of one of his father's vivid literary portraits of tangled legal life, Dickens Jr found himself presiding for some hours over the ceremony. This was because, as the *Times* of 12 January 1921 under the headline 'NERVOUS WOMEN JURORS' reported, 'many women sought to be excused'. The first lady called asked to be released on the grounds that she was unable to leave her 83-year-old mother. The fourth was excused because she had no one to look after her tobacconist business. When another woman's name was called, her daughter came forward and said that her mother was 80, and others were also excused on the grounds of age. Dickens told a woman of 61 that 65 was the age limit, but he released her for reasons of ill health. Then, reported the *Times*, there was the following exchange:

Woman juror: 'I am so awfully nervous I don't think I am suitable.'
The Common Serjeant: 'We are all more or less nervous.'
Woman juror: 'I should feel most grateful if you could excuse me.'
The Common Serjeant: 'Don't you think you could sit quietly in that box and listen? There is not much to make you nervous. You won't be cross-examined there,

you know. [Laughter.] If I accepted your excuse I don't think I should get any ladies at all.'

Woman juror: 'I am sure there are numbers who would enjoy it …'

The Common Serjeant: 'Who are more strong-minded than yourself?'

Woman juror: 'Yes.'

She was excused. Next was a woman who wished to be stood down because she claimed she had to look after her workpeople in a factory. Dickens told her it was her 'public duty' to let her work stand aside for a time. 'If people were excluded simply because they are employers of labour, we should hardly get a jury at all. Perhaps you would like to serve later?' To which she retorted, much to the court's merriment, 'Well, if I have got to serve, I would rather serve now.' In all, about half of the originally summoned 50 were finally excused.

According to the *Manchester Guardian*: 'One of the more experienced women before going into court said that she did not expect to like the work, but she thought it was very necessary that women should take their share in public life and in all civic duties. She believed, too, that the presence of women on juries would result in greater care being taken in cases where women were concerned. Some cases would be very unpleasant, but men had not shirked their duties and women must equally show a public spirit.'

The first mixed Old Bailey jury comprised just two women who, noted the *Manchester Guardian*, took the oath in voices 'clear and steady'. They sat in the more senior Recorder's Court and tried two cases, each one resulting in an acquittal. In Dickens' court, just one woman was selected for jury service that day, the splendidly named Mrs Taylor Bumstead, who, befitting her formidable moniker, was made 'Forewoman'. She was also involved in two cases, the first concerning two Danes who were charged with shooting at a policeman and acquitted; the second involved a man charged with wounding his wife. He was convicted and sentenced to six months' imprisonment in the second division, a legal classification from 1898 which avoided hard labour.

Talking to the *Times* after the cases, Mrs Bumstead said she had found her experience 'extremely interesting', adding, 'I was sorry that the man in the second case was sent to prison, but I was glad it was in the second division so that he does not lose his pension. I thought the police officer very humane in speaking up for him as he did.' Apparently a veteran of public life, she also concluded boldly, 'Women jurors should be provided with refreshment during the day or their expenses should be refunded. It cost me 6s today for expenses and, as I am to be here for seven days, it looks as if my first experience as a juror will prove somewhat expensive to me.'

It's perhaps interesting to note that, while the Recorder and his Clerk used the address 'Ladies and Gentlemen of the jury' in their court, the Common Serjeant and his Clerk settled for the simpler 'Members of the jury'.

Out in the shires, the novelty continued to confuse. At Huntingdon Assizes, where three women were serving, Captain Falcon MP, who was appearing in a case, began by addressing the jury as 'Ladies and Gentlemen of the jury' only to be swiftly admonished by the Judge, who told him that 'Members of the jury' was the 'proper form of address', before adding tartly, 'You're not making an after-dinner speech!'

A day after the Old Bailey bastion was breached, and a day before Bailey's trial was due to begin at Aylesbury, presided over by Mr Justice McCardie, *Punch*, the weekly magazine of humour and satire, decided to cash in on the novelty of women jurors with a poem called 'Trial by Jury – New Style' in its Miscellany column, *Charivari*, following this preamble, or news 'hook': 'During the hearing of a recent case, one of the jury produced her knitting in the box. If this thing is done in open court, the poet trembles to think what may happen when the jury retires to consider their verdict.' The poem ran as follows:

''Tis time,' the foreman said, 'to weigh
The question of his guilt;
The case to me, I'm bound to say.
Seems proven to the hilt.'
But mid the twelve true souls and good
One spoke in doubting strain:
'The question puzzling me is should
The next be purl or plain.'

In such a complicated key
Her pattern had been planned
The case was one that could not be
Decided out of hand;
For many an hour they sought in vain
Its mystery to unfurl
For six said 'Guilty,' four said 'Plain'
And two stuck out for 'Purl.'

The Judge sent out to ask them if
His light on some dark spot
Would help them: with a scornful sniff
They answered it would not;

And, though the felon's guilt was black
(Past doubt he did the deed)
They had at last to put him back —
The jury disagreed.

If this all sounds just faintly patronising, then *Punch* would go at least some way to rectifying the matter exactly a week later, in its 19 January edition, with a very respectful full-length cartoon drawn by Bernard Partridge, one of its more distinguished contributors. Entitled 'The Chief's Last Charge', it depicted 'The New Viceroy of India (the departing Lord Chief Justice, Rufus Isaacs, Earl of Reading) saying to 'the New Juror', an elegantly clad and fashionably hatted woman, 'Madam. I could not leave the cause of justice in fairer hands.'

Just over a week later, when you might have thought the novelty had worn off, the courts and newspaper columns were once again full of concern about mixed juries. It seems that no sooner had Mr Justice McCardie come away from his assignment in Aylesbury than he was pontificating on the subject at Leicester Assizes in a case of alleged rape where three women jurors had been challenged by the Counsel for the Defence. The *Times* reported on 28 January, '[he] said his reason was that a case of this kind should be tried by a jury of either all men or all women. There were unpleasant details which could not frankly be discussed by a mixed jury.'

His Lordship clearly had much sympathy with the objection and said he was glad Counsel had mounted the challenge. 'Women jurors must retire, but there was no reflection as to their capacity.' He thought the time was near 'when Parliament must consider whether a mixed jury was the best tribunal to try a case where, if a proper decision were to be arrived at, there was involved full and frank discussion of many intimate sexual details.' He then, concluded the report, 'assured the women that there was no other ground for objecting to them'.

If trying a case of alleged rape wasn't bad enough, then having a mixed jury – or women jurors period, for that matter – subjected to the shocking vagaries of the Divorce Court would seem positively beyond the pale judging by an extraordinary correspondence that then ensued across several days in the *Times* following some controversial cross-suits in that division of the High Court.

Writing from the Garrick Club, Lt Col CP Hawkes spluttered, 'That women, presumably of refined feelings and sensibilities, should be compulsorily and publicly subjected to the revelation of the most revolting and degrading indecencies as a necessary part of a public duty which the majority of them neither desired not demanded, cannot seriously have been contemplated even by our enlightened Legislature.'

Calling himself 'a Barrister', another wrote, even more intemperately, 'It is revolting that women should now be obliged to discuss, when considering their verdict, with members of the opposite sex who are total strangers to them, certain matters which no decent woman would for one moment think of mentioning even to her husband.'

He then added, 'It may be urged that, as women demanded the vote, they must, therefore, accept all the responsibilities which enfranchisement entails. It must, however, be remembered that women were not consulted as a whole on the subject, and were they consulted today I have little doubt there would be a great majority against jury service at all events in the [Divorce and Criminal] Courts I have mentioned.' It was nothing less than 'a blot on the administration of justice', which, he concluded, should be hastily removed.

His assumption about women and their alleged view of jury service would seem at the very least condescending until one then read, three days later, a flurry of letters, which assuming their veracity appeared to give him some credence. 'I know a great deal about my sister-voters who are labouring day after day, cooking, sweeping, dusting and ironing that they may stand between their men folk and discomforts in the home,' declared 'Home-working woman', who continued in a similar vein: 'They recognise the truth that though women are gifted in many ways, they are not just, that they lack knowledge of the law, and that some are ignorant of sin and crime. These women look to their men folk to stand between them and the discomforts of such tasks as serving upon a jury.'

She then urged an amendment of the Act, 'so worded that no woman need serve on a jury against her will'. Her plea was underscored by 'Mother of eight' who beseeched, 'We ask at least to have all compulsion done away with, and we appeal to men to do this for us. All down the ages we have looked to men to protect us; surely they will not fail us now?'

However, when it seemed that the cause of women's suffrage had been done irreparable damage by these oddly revisionist outbursts, there was by way of counterpoint a considerably saner summation by Mrs JH Woodward, who wrote, almost philosophically, 'To have the vote, to act on juries, to enter the Bar – all this is only of value if it is to be the means to one end, and that is a purer life – a more healthy because a more moral country.'

Yet, just a week before this fracas came news from the States that would, and should, surely have been food for thought – the first criminal trial in America presided over by a woman Judge. In Cleveland Ohio, the *New York Herald* reported that Justice Florence Allen passed a sentence of life imprisonment on Robert Comens for 'murder in the second degree' after a trial – almost contemporaneous with proceedings at Aylesbury – that had included three women on the jury. Two of them had pleaded to be excused from duty because of their husbands' objections and the demands of their children. 'Justice Allen, a spinster,' wrote the *New York Herald*, 'declared, however, that the existence of husbands and children was no excuse.'

In the mother country, though, it would take another 40 years for the first female Judge to be appointed – Elizabeth Lane to the County Court in 1962 – and another ten years after that for Rose Heilbron to become the first female Judge to preside at the Old Bailey, on 4 January 1972.

Meanwhile, on the morning of 13 January 1921, Miss Maud Sophia Stevenson, Miss Annie Anderson White and Miss Matilda Polly Tack were creating their own significant piece of English legal history when they first stepped into the jury box at Bucks Assizes.

4

NO ORDINARY TRIAL:
DAY ONE

Like some sinister playbill, the Calendar of Prisoners proclaimed the list of defendants awaiting trial at Quarter Sessions and Assizes, and the respective charges against them. In addition to Bailey, on the Calendar for the Winter Assizes at Aylesbury in the County of Buckingham beginning 12 January 1921 before The Hon Sir Henry Alfred McCardie Kt were four other prisoners: John Thomas Tiller, 41, accused of 'unlawfully and carnally knowing' his 13-year-old daughter Violet; Florence North, 18, accused of perjury; Charles Edwin New, 30, a piano tuner, said to have stolen a purse containing about 18s; and Joseph Bassett, alias Joseph Foskett, a 45-year-old plateman who was alleged to have indulged in a veritable crime spree, consisting of the theft of a bicycle, cash box containing £2, War Bonds worth £110, War Savings Certificates to the value of 15s 6d each, a number of antique and Roman coins, and a metal cash box containing about 5s in coppers.

But quite clearly top of the bill was Bailey, charged not only with murder but also, according to the Calendar, that 'on the 30th day of September 1920 at Little Marlow, feloniously and violently did assault Lilian Pretoria Rose Marks and then did attempt violently and against her will to ravish and carnally know the said Lilian Pretoria Rose Marks'.

What better stage for the denouement of this tasty selection of alleged crime and criminals than Aylesbury's County Hall, originally built in the early 18th century to designs approved by Sir John Vanbrugh? It was originally intended primarily as the county gaol but also boasted two courtrooms and offices for the Clerk of the Peace, later to include the County Council Chamber.

Bucks Assizes had long been the arena for some locally famous murder cases, after which, up to and including the sensational case of John Tawell in 1845 who was accused of poisoning his mistress, convicted killers might as likely be hanged from a rope tied with three half hitches on the county hall balcony overlooking the town's Market Square while witnessed by a baying mob.

Ironically, perhaps the most famous case of all to be heard, in part at least, in this venerable building was not a murder at all but that of the Great Train Robbers in 1964. However, the courtroom wasn't deemed big enough to accommodate the proceedings so the trial had to be switched to the offices of Aylesbury Rural District Council nearby, returning to the old County Hall for the sentencing only.

Six years later, 18-year-old Paul Stanislaw Dabrowski walked into County Hall, doused it with petrol and set the place ablaze. It seems that Dabrowski and his younger brother had appeared in the court as children and had been sentenced for minor offences. Mentally unbalanced and contemplating suicide, he had decided to confront his grief and despair by taking it out on the building – but not before removing the New Testament from the witness box to stop it from being burned. He would go on to serve 11 years in Broadmoor, Rampton and other secure units before eventually being released in the early 1980s. Meanwhile, just 12 months and £200,000 later, the Court and the Council Chamber were back in business restored as closely as possible to their original form following the fire which had engulfed almost all the building apart from a small section of panelling and a shield bearing a royal coat of arms.

Almost exactly 50 years earlier, it was into the dock of the original, Vanbrugh-approved, courtroom that at 2.25pm on the second day of the Assizes, in the matter of Rex v George Arthur Bailey, the defendant stepped confidently, flanked by two warders. The Clerk, George Pleydell Bancroft, then read out, 'George Arthur Bailey, you stand charged upon this indictment, and upon the Coroner's inquisition, with the murder of Kate Lilian Bailey on the 29 September last year. Are you guilty or not guilty?'

In a firm and clear voice, Bailey replied, 'Not guilty.'

There was, however, no mention now of the other lesser, albeit still grave, charge against Bailey that had decorated the published Calendar. Until the last ten years or so, the practice in English courts was that, if a man or woman was charged with murder, then whatever else they had done, the indictment at trial would contain a single count of murder. It was generally felt that such a charge was so grave that it would be unfair for a defendant to have to defend himself against other allegations at the same time.

Bailey had, in fact, arrived in Aylesbury from Oxford by train some hours earlier, around 10.15am, but because another of the cases on the Calendar hadn't been completed he had been confined to the cells beneath the Court under the watchful eye of the warders who'd brought him across country that morning. He was probably not aware of the fact that, according to the *Bucks Free Press*, there was 'outside the Court a long queue of sightseers, the majority clamouring for admission in the hope of hearing the sordid story unfolded'.

Bailey's state of mind as he prepared himself for trial, preparation for which included reading and re-reading the papers of earlier proceedings at Marlow Police Court and the inquest as well as their press reports, might possibly have been detected in a poem he had completed and handed to his solicitor on 7 January:

> *Buffeted, clinging to straws, straws rotating,*
> *Straws weak, straws broken, vainly plotting;*
> *Plotting, planning, beating against the surge,*
> *Gasping, sinking, striving to emerge,*
> *To make one giant bid for hopeless cause;*
> *Yet dare I not complain – inscrutable.*
> *The ways of God are far beyond our ken;*
> *I bow to Thy decree, O God: remorse.*
> *Yes, for the past, but resigned to Thee.*
> *Life given, life lost, but life retained,*
> *Life's failure, yet the end attained –*
> *Thy inviolable decree.*
> *From off the narrow way, our paths yet still converging.*
> *Though broad the track, in circles wayward trending;*
> *Still there is 'God', to Whom all roads are wending.*
> *The narrow way, the narrow gate, Eternity unending.*

His official 'state of mind' was summed up in a note by Oxford Prison's Medical Officer, Dr RH Sankey MB, who wrote five days before the trial was due to begin: 'This prisoner has been under observation since he was committed to this prison. He is certainly very peculiar but I do not consider him to be certifiable as insane. He is fit to plead.'

Eventually 'put up' after the lunch break, Bailey, noticeably pale-faced, would have glanced around the dimly lit Assize Court to discover it 'packed to its utmost capacity, many ladies being present, both in the gallery and in the well of the Court. The space usually allotted to the press was allocated to ticket holders.'

The Clerk told Bailey that he was going to read out the names of the jury and that he had the right to object before they were sworn in. It wasn't, however, to be an objection from Bailey which first rang around the court, but from Miss Maud Stevenson, one of the three women jurors who were about to make history. 'By reason of the evidence which will come before the jury in this case, I would rather not serve,' she declared, before adding, 'I do not wish to shirk my public duties and responsibilities.'

His Lordship observed, 'I am afraid that there is no rule that a person may object upon the ground that they would not care to listen to the evidence.'

Miss Stevenson retorted, 'I understand it lies within the power of your Lordship.'

The Prosecuting Counsel, Mr Young, stood and declared, 'So far as the Prosecution are concerned, I am quite willing that she shall stand down, apart from any ruling as to whether she shall stand aside.'

For the Defence, Mr Johnston said, 'The Defence will have no objection.'

'If you have an essential objection to serving,' His Lordship added, 'I am quite willing to listen to it, but I am afraid I cannot grant exemption on the grounds you mention.'

Miss Stevenson was then forced to concede. 'If you wish it, I am willing to do the same as the others.'

His Lordship continued, 'I am afraid that the point that you raise is one of important principle. If ladies are to be excused from service upon juries because they feel the evidence may cause them pain or distress, it would involve this, that many ladies might escape altogether from that which is a duty imposed upon them by the Jury Act, that they together with men should discharge the functions of a jury. I could not accede to your request without establishing a precedent, which might not be to the best interest of the public. I am afraid, therefore, that I cannot excuse you on that ground.'

Miss Stevenson was duly sworn.

What of the other principal players in this drama? Leading the case for the Crown was Mr Hugo Young KC, at 73, a veteran barrister of almost 50 years' experience since being first 'called' in 1872. A man of Lincolnshire, he took immense pride that he was, at the time of the trial, also Recorder of Lincoln, in the county of his birth. He especially delighted in the fact that, during the 15 years of his Recordership, not one of his decisions had ever been overruled by a Court of Appeal.

Compared with Young's immense judicial experience, both in Court and on the Bench, Mr Johnston, appearing for the Defence, aged 35, was a veritable novice, although they did share membership of the same Inn of Court, Inner Temple.

The son of a doctor, Leicester-born Samuel Frederick Sinclair Johnston attended Rossall School in Lancashire before winning a scholarship to Trinity College, Oxford in 1904. The tutorial register records that Johnston took part one of a Classics degree before resigning to take up Law. He qualified as a barrister in 1909 but, when war was declared in 1914, he joined up almost immediately in the Royal Army Service Corps. Johnston served for the duration, rising to Captain and earning a 'mention in dispatches'. There is also record of him being awarded a medal (which he didn't actually receive until 1923, just two years before he would die tragically of TB in a Swiss sanatorium when aged barely 40).

Presiding over the trial was 51-year-old Mr Justice McCardie, a popular albeit controversial figure who had been a Judge of the High Court since 1916, but, like the opposing Counsel, was born and raised in the provinces of firmly middle-class stock.

Mr Young, a rather owlish-looking man with a beak of a nose, began, in what was described as 'an even, conversational tone', to outline the case for the Prosecution in a two-hour opening speech. He had just finished reading Bailey's letter to the Coroner when the Judge interrupted him with a crucial piece of housekeeping. He told the jury that the case would probably go on until Saturday, and that they wouldn't be able to go home that night but would have to be kept together. If they wished, he would adjourn the Court for a few minutes so they could telegraph family or friends and he would make sure they were supplied with paper, pen and ink by Court officials. Most of the jury took advantage of this concession during a brief break.

Resuming, Mr Young moved on to Bailey's system of musical notation and read out the two advertisements for young ladies, placed two months apart in the local paper. It was Bailey's ambition to get rid of his wife and for his own immoral purposes he wanted to engage young women, the Crown said.

At which, Mr Johnston quickly rose to his feet arguing that this evidence was inadmissible on the grounds that the prisoner's motive in respect of the young ladies was not necessarily evidence of motive for murdering his wife. He then suggested firmly that the point should be discussed further in the absence of the jury. The Judge agreed and the jury left the Court.

For his part, Mr Young said that it was material to the question of motive to show that part of Bailey's scheme was to get girls into his house for unlawful purposes, and he proposed to show that, in the case of Miss Marks, Bailey went to her room at night and made proposals to her, which she resented, and he refused to leave the bedroom. Another contention was that Bailey intended to have a riotous week and then end his own life.

The Judge added that the case for the Crown was that, if the prisoner's wife had remained in the house alive, Bailey could not have embarked upon 'the other efforts', for the success of which the death of his wife was a necessary object. Moreover, said the Judge, some of Bailey's statements to Miss Marks might be distinctly relevant to the case. For instance, when Bailey said, 'I want you to be mistress of the cottage,' he must have been aware his wife was dead.

What soon became crystal clear was that, despite the fact that the second charge against Bailey had now been officially dropped, evidence around it would, as the Judge then confirmed, be deemed admissible to prove motive.

The jury filed back into Court again to hear Mr Young conclude by reading out Bailey's voluntary statement to Marlow Police on 12 October. There were many acts which, said Counsel, suggested Bailey knew exactly what he was doing. That he was 'a peculiar man' in some respects, there could be no doubt, added Mr Young, as he resumed his seat with the courtroom clock showing 4.45pm.

The final half hour of these opening salvoes was taken up with evidence from five witnesses including Inspector West, Supt Kirby and the two doctors, Dr Wills and Dr Dunbar Dickson, who'd been summoned by the police to examine it.

Inspector West was then cross-examined by Mr Johnston, who asked, 'I do not quite follow what you said about the position of the body. Do I understand that the body was lying under the bed wrapped in a sheet?'

'Yes,' replied Inspector West. 'Hanging down from the bed there was a counterpane. The body was wrapped up in a sheet, and the bed was on top of the body. There were two counterpanes. One was hanging down by the side of the bed, and the other was hanging long ways. I found nothing on the body but a sheet and some underclothing.'

'There were no other clothes on the body?'

'No.'

According to Dr Wills, Kate's body was also clad in a nightdress. He also said that, when the body was turned over, the red fluid, which came out of her mouth, had 'the odour of almonds'. Did Dr Dickson notice the almond smell?

'I did not,' he told Mr Young. He also confirmed that the body was stiff when he examined it.

On which bleak note, Court was then adjourned for the day.

What of Bailey's demeanour in the dock during that first afternoon? He had listened attentively, the local papers reported, and even raised 'the ghost of smile' when Mr Young, in his opening, referred to the fact that one of the witnesses had, at a previous hearing, described the prisoner's music notation as 'grotesque'.

As Mr Justice McCardie crossed the gallery from the back of the Court to the well-appointed Judge's Lodgings – replete with bedrooms and excellent dining room under the supervision of a resident housekeeper – to settle in for the night, the jury made its way out of the building, across Market Square and up to the nearby Bull's Head Hotel where they were to be lodged for the night and for as many more nights as the trial might require. At the hotel, where their host was the genial Signor Giacomo Eugenio Atturro Gargini (from a long-established family line of innkeepers), the jury were attended by Mrs Noble, a woman usher – yet another innovation.

'The three women jurors,' the *Times* would report gravely the following day, 'had the novel experience of being "locked up" with the men of the jury at a local hotel. It is the custom in murder trials for the juries to be kept together in this way, under the surveillance of an Officer of the Court, to prevent communication with the public. On this occasion, the whole of the hotel accommodation was placed at the jury's disposal, and special arrangements were made for the comfort of the women members.'

Quite what these 'special arrangements' actually were is not recorded. One hopes they at least took full advantage of the first-class hotel's facilities, which included a restaurant, palm court, billiard saloon and oyster bar.

5

MUSIC, MADNESS
AND MURDER:
DAY TWO

'Sensation followed sensation as the whole story was unfolded of the Barn Cottage Poison Drama'. Cut off in midstream, as it were, the previous Friday just one day into the trial, the weekly *Bucks Free Press* clearly felt it had to make up for lost time the following Friday, 21 January, with pages of lavish, not to say hyperbolic, coverage four days *after* the verdict was in. What the paper surely cannot have anticipated in its reporting on 14 January was that, at the beginning of Day Two, just as copies of the latest edition were being snapped up across the county, the *BFP* was effectively, albeit briefly, in the dock itself.

As Court resumed at 10.30am, Mr Young was instantly on his feet addressing the Judge, saying, 'My lord, before we begin this morning I want to mention a thing which had been brought to my notice. A newspaper called the *Bucks Free Press*, published this morning, has thought fit to publish certain letters which were not put in evidence yesterday and, as far as I know, may not be put in evidence at all. I wanted to say that I think the jury – if they have not had an opportunity of seeing the paper – should be cautioned against reading it today, or until the trial is over.'

He was referring in particular to the publication of Kate's note of desperation to her mother, under the sub-heading 'A Letter', which had last been produced in evidence at the adjourned inquest back at the end of November. The note had once again been reproduced in full, together with Bailey's vivid statement to Marlow Magistrates emphatically denying the charges, bracketed together in the paper as a kind of trailer for their readers the following week rather in the manner of one of those 'Previously ...' recaps so beloved of television soap-opera producers these days.

'The jury, probably, have not seen the paper,' snorted Mr Justice McCardie, before Mr Johnston chipped in swiftly with: 'The solicitors for the Defence state that they have nothing to do with the insertion of the letter. I am informed that this letter was actually printed in the report of the Coroner's inquest.'

Then, with the representatives of the *Bucks Free Press* doubtless quaking in their boots, the Judge carefully spelled out the potential consequences. 'I am glad Mr Hugo Young has called my attention to this. It is most important that nothing should be published either locally or otherwise which has not transpired in the course of this trial. If any publication does take place otherwise than that which has occurred in Court, it would be his duty to indicate to the authorities in order that a motion to commit for contempt of Court may be made to the King's Bench Division. If that motion be made, I do not doubt that the Court will find it their duty to send to prison those who have gravely infringed the elementary rules of justice.'

The Judge asked the jury if they'd seen that day's edition of the paper, to which they firmly replied, 'No,' adding that they hadn't seen the letter either. Supt Kirby and Mr Woodward, one of the Defence solicitors, also informed the Judge that the letter had been previously read in public. All of which seemed perfectly to satisfy His Lordship. The publishers of the *Bucks Free Press* were duly, in the paper's own, relieved, words, 'exonerated from any blame'.

After that distraction, the Prosecution case continued with the arrival in the witness box of Edwin Hall, the Bourne End dairyman, who took on Bailey after the prisoner had replied to his advertisement in the national farming press for a roundsman, to deliver milk and other dairy goods in the Bourne End and Little Marlow area.

In cross-examination, Hall confirmed that Bailey had made a success of his round with which the dairyman had had some difficulties before the prisoner took it over.

'He was quite popular, and quite a well-known character?' asked Mr Johnston.

'Yes.'

'He was [sometimes] called "The Whistling Milkman", was he not?'

'Yes.'

As far as Bailey's illness was concerned, Hall understood that it involved an abscess on the side of the face, which was, although he hadn't seen it himself, strapped up. When he did see him early on during this latter period, Bailey, said Hall, 'certainly did look very ill'.

In a crossfire of further questions from Defence Counsel as

well as the Judge and Mr Young, Hall said he had seen Kate on or around 20 September looking in 'very good health', that he thought he remembered seeing Bailey with a plaster on his cheek, or somehow 'bandaged up', and that he'd sent the prisoner a message saying he couldn't let him be off duty for too long and that he might have to fill his place. And, no, he hadn't heard (until mention of it in the first letter) about any problem with Bailey's 'lungs'.

The Court next heard from Miss Mary Hillary, the owner of Millbrook in Furlong Road, Bourne End, which she rented to Bailey when he moved to the town to take up his new job. At first, she explained from the witness box, he lived there on his own along with two or three other lodgers. In July, he wrote to her asking if he could rent the whole place furnished because he wanted to have his wife and child live there with him. Also, would she object if they shared with another couple called Roper who had two children? She also said that Bailey had complained about an ants' nest near the larder.

Had, the Judge asked, Bailey ever complained about wasps' nests in the walls of the house? 'No,' she said, adding that she'd never seen one herself. As for those pesky ants, there were cracks in the kitchen through which ants might emerge, though she hadn't seen any herself.

'There might have been?' asked Mr Johnston.

'There might be,' she replied.

'Have you ever poured a kettle of boiling water down the cracks?' Mr Young asked.

'Yes, lots of times.'

'What does that do to the ants?'

'Nothing,' was the reply, as the Court dissolved into laughter.

In September, there was, said Miss Hillary, a disagreement

over rent and Bailey moved on, fatefully, to Barn Cottage after he'd answered an ad inserted in the local paper by Miss Alice Boney, daughter of the property's owner.

After getting her to confirm details of the inside and outside of the cottage as well as surroundings, including yard, barn and garden, along with its proximity to neighbouring properties and the river, Miss Boney was asked if she noticed any wasps on the couple of occasions she'd visited Barn Cottage in August. No, she hadn't. The Judge then asked if she'd spotted any wasps' nests. Again, no, although she did recall one from the summer before. She'd also never received any complaints from Bailey about wasps.

It was now the moment to hear for the first time from some of Bailey's more immediate family – his sister Helen and her husband Jim Jennings, an iron foundryman, who had travelled to Aylesbury from their home in Swindon. Mr Jennings was first to give evidence and he told the Court that he'd seen Bailey on 30 September around 8.00pm at their home, where the prisoner had just arrived with Hollie. Bailey told him that Kate was 'in Wycombe hospital for a premature birth'. The following day, Jennings saw him briefly when he returned for his lunch and Bailey told him he was going to return to Little Marlow to check how Kate was. However, Bailey was still in Swindon that evening when his brother-in-law came home from work. This time, Bailey told him that Kate was dead, while Jennings was given to believe that Bailey had been to Little Marlow and back during the day.

'Was there any talk about insurance?' the Prosecution asked him.

'I mentioned, "Have you got your wife insured, George?" and he said, "I would rather have my wife than all the insurance."'

In cross-examination, he told Mr Johnston he had known Bailey since 1913 and that, as far as he knew, he and Kate were indeed, according to Counsel's questions, 'a most affectionate and happy couple' and 'quite wrapped up in each other'. What he didn't know anything about was Bailey's musical system. Had he ever heard the system being mentioned? the Judge asked him.

'Not to me.'

'Never?'

'No, sir.'

'You and he did not have much in common lately?' Mr Justice McCardie reflected sardonically.

'No.'

Helen, known as Nellie, Jennings took the stand and, like her husband, she said she saw Bailey when he and Hollie turned up at their home on 30 September and told her about Kate being hospitalised in Wycombe; it was the first time she'd seen him since June when he'd left Swindon to take up the roundsman's job in Bourne End. In early September, however, she had written to her brother sending him £3 towards their advance rent at Barn Cottage. Her accompanying letter, though containing some incomprehensible references, provides an intriguing snapshot of the times:

> *Dear George and Kitty* [her name for Kate],
> *Thank you for the box of flowers received on Monday. Some of them were no good, but I could see what beauties they were when freshly cut from the garden. I expect you were disappointed over the Carnival. Well, now, I have been very undecided all the week about the money, for I have been thinking about Coal Strike* [which started on 18 October]; *but it seems more hopeful now. Thank God for that. And I have my poor old boy home*

very queer this week. He started Monday morning to show willing, but he had to have a pass out at half-past nine o'clock. He went up to the doctor's, and he soon told him he was not to go to work for a few days at least. To have a thorough rest, so we shall not get any money next week.

But any rate I have saved £3 since Jim has been doing a bit of piece work whilst two of his mates were out ill. So I am sending it on to you to enable you to get the house as I know it is an awful how-to-do about houses now. Kitty said in her letter that if I could manage £3 you could manage the other, so I hope it will enable you to advance the rent.

Victor is very queer: a nasty rash all over his body, but there you know not any of us have really been well for long at a time since we came back here; we miss the pure air of the fields and the old brook. Well, at any rate, that is what I think. Now I hope little Hollie didn't bruise her poor little head much, for you never know what these knocks will lead to.

I will come up and see you when things have settled down again. Let me know if you receive the money alright. Trusting you are all keeping well. I have polished the tables and chairs, and to tell the truth I should be sorry to see them go again. If you find the bed a nuisance you could sell the bedstead and palliasses, and send the flock bed back to me if you like. I expect you find it better to go into furnished rooms then bother about furniture.

Well, old dears, I will stop, as I am doing all sorts of jobs today, pickling, washing etc. Give Hollie a big kiss from us all, and love for yourselves. Goodbyee.

From your loving sister, Nellie. My nib is a beast.

On 1 October, Bailey told her that he was going back to Buckinghamshire to check on Kate.

'At what time did he leave your house?' the Prosecution asked.

'About 1.15pm.'

'What time did he return?'

'5.15pm.'

'When he came in, what did he say?'

'"For God's sake, don't tell her," meaning the child.'

'What did you say?'

'I said, "Has the worst happened, George?"'

'What did he reply?'

'He said, "She died at three o'clock this morning."'

'How did he appear then?'

'Very overcome and very upset.'

Bailey left the Jennings' home the following morning, 2 October, shortly before 10.30am, leaving Hollie with them.

Cross-examined by Mr Johnston, Helen was asked to give the Court some details of her brother's life and family background, including the illnesses and injuries he suffered at various stages. She had just got to the point of explaining about a steel and leather contraption he wore on his knee, when the Judge suddenly intervened.

'Is it true,' he barked, 'that someone is using a camera in Court, and taking photographs of the prisoner? Will the police officer go up and prevent anyone from passing from the gallery. I am told photographs are being taken of the prisoner in the dock. I do not want to have any person searched, but I shall not hesitate to make that order if there is any continuation of the photographing which was about to take place.'

He also ordered the doors to be closed if there was any denial of the accusation while a thorough search was carried out. The Under-Sheriff, a senior police officer and one of the ushers then made their way up to the gallery to confront the offending snappers.

After a brief hiatus, the Judge asked, 'What is the result of the search?'

He was told that two cameras had been seized; in one case, five plates had been handed over; in the other, seven plates. The names of the photographers were also taken.

'I regret,' said the Judge, 'that photographs have been taken by those who have received accommodation in this Court this morning. I shall not hesitate to give in to custody any person who breaks the rules of the Court by photographing a prisoner in the dock or any other person in Court. Judges have often pointed out the cruelty of placing in the public press for the benefit of a merely curious public the features of a man who is undergoing the mental torture of a trial which may or may not result in the gravest possible consequences to himself. I shall not commit those persons to whom my attention has been called, but if there is any repetition of the offence I shall at once send the offenders to prison.'

Mr Young thought His Lordship should know that 'there have appeared photographs of the prisoner, and also of the lady portion of the jury'.

Mr Justice McCardie replied, smiling, 'I do not think that is the gravest portion.'

Later that day, after the cameras' plates had been rendered useless, they, together with the cameras, were returned to the two photographers who were held for a while in the gallery until the Court had been entirely cleared.

Meanwhile, Helen Jennings had continued, via the careful questioning of Mr Johnston, to provide a vivid portrait of her brother.

'When the prisoner was a boy at school, what was his general health like?'

'Fairly well. He was in very good health, but peculiar at times.'

'Do you mean queer?'

'A little queer in his head. He was never the same as the rest of us.'

'How did he show his peculiarity?'

'In all sorts of ways. He was queer, and his health became bad.'

'How did he seem peculiar?' chipped in the Judge. 'What did you notice about him?'

No answer at first, so the Judge asked her again.

'As a boy, he sat a lot by himself and moped over different things.'

'He was not stupid?' asked Mr Johnston.

'No. He was the clever one, and he had to leave school through that.'

'Did he leave school through cleverness?'

'He had reached the highest standard there was.'

'He got to it before boys his age generally get there?'

'Yes.'

She said she remembered being told that he had tried to commit suicide – 'ten or eleven years ago; it must be some time, when I was a young girl myself'. Then there was an occasion in February 1913 after he'd had a nervous breakdown – 'I know he was found somewhere, but I could not tell you where. I heard something of it a few months after.'

And had he also tried to take his own life again, Mr Johnston asked, about the time Kate was expecting her first baby?

'Yes, I was told he did.'

'Was that also with poison?'

'I could not tell you, sir.'

'You have told us about the attempts at suicide. Do you know anything about any of these instances, except what you may have heard from other people?' asked Mr Young, re-examining.

'I know only what I heard from my mother. She told me.'

'Did any other relatives tell you?' interjected the Judge.

'My oldest sister.'

'They told you that which you have told us?'

'Yes.'

'You never were present with him in the house at the time when he was suffering from these alleged attempts at suicide?' continued Mr Young.

'No.'

The Court also heard how Bailey as 'a young lad' would write plays and poetry. Then, later on, there was, of course, the invention of a system of musical notation.

'He was always musical, was he not?' Mr Johnston asked.

Yes, he was always musical.'

'From quite a boy?'

'Yes.'

'Could he play the piano?'

'He could play it by ear.'

'He could play the zither, mandolin and other small instruments?'

'Yes, and the banjo.'

Then, contriving one of the most curious non-sequiturs that could ever be envisaged, Mr Johnston said, 'I am going to ask you one more question that may cause you pain. Did the prisoner's father die of acute melancholia?'

'Yes.'

In his re-examination of the witness, Mr Young mused suggestively how it could be possible for a man who urgently needed money for rent to be able also to be planning to pay young women three guineas a week to copy his notation system. He also wanted Helen Jennings to be a bit more specific about her brother's so-called playwriting skills and supposed musical prowess.

'Now, about the plays. Did he ever have any of these plays produced at any theatre?'

'No.'

'Did he write plays?'

'I remember him writing one, but I did not understand it.'

'You did not regard it as a sign of weakness of mind?'

'No.'

'Now, about his music. As far as you know, was he ever much of a musician?'

'No, he was not.'

'Did he play?'

'He used to play by ear.'

'You never saw him with a piece of music in front of him at the piano?'

'No.'

'He would sit down at the piano, and what you would call "vamp"?'

'Yes.'

'You said the system was complete?' She had previously answered that this was so when questioned by Mr Johnston.

'I do not know quite what you mean by that.'

'That was the word that was put into your mouth?'

'Yes, I understood my brother to say it was.'

She was then shown some copies of Bailey's notation,

which had been made by the 'young ladies' in question to illustrate and teach the system.

'Can you read music?' asked the Judge.

'No,' she replied.

Now it was His Lordship's turn to change tack dramatically as he suddenly queried, 'Is your mother here?'

'No,' she said, revealing she was the only member of six surviving siblings (a brother had died in the war) to be present in Court. As Helen Jennings' evidence about suicide attempts was purely based on hearsay, the Judge asked if it was possible that Bailey's mother, who lived in north Devon, could attend the trial and directed that the police should get in touch as soon as possible with the police in Ilfracombe to facilitate that. Later that day, the Court would hear back that 67-year-old Mrs Bailey was suffering from bronchitis and pleurisy; she was deemed too unwell to travel.

'Was your mother ashamed of these attempts at suicide?' Mr Johnston asked her.

'Yes.'

'Did she regard them as a credit to the family?'

'No. Good gracious not.'

'She never mentioned it at all?'

'I don't suppose she did.'

'She kept it as quiet as she could?'

'Yes.'

It was during his sister's evidence that the first significant chinks in Bailey's formidable composure finally emerged as he appeared to break down, at times quite clearly wiping tears from his eyes. Before Helen Jennings left the witness box, the Judge asked Mr Johnston if he was 'coming to the issue as to the state of mind of this man, the prisoner, at the time this offence was committed, to show the legal responsibility for the act'.

Counsel replied rather non-committally, 'That is a point to be considered.'

In fact, Helen was recalled later that morning and asked if one of her other brothers, Thomas, who lived in West Hampstead, might be able to help on the matter of the suicide attempts.

'Would he not know almost as much as your mother?' the Judge asked her.

'No doubt he very likely would.'

'Pray get Thomas Bailey here.'

There followed the evidence of three police officers – PC Henry Poole, stationed at Marlow, Sergeant Oliver Purdy from Reading, and Supt Kirby of High Wycombe – who, variously, gave the Court details about the discovery of Kate's body and then the subsequent detention, questioning and arrest of Bailey, who had been found with various bottled poisons about his person. This was also the perfect juncture for the official introduction at Aylesbury of Bailey's notorious letter to the Coroner, which was read out in Court by the Clerk.

The question of those poisons and how they were at first obtained by Bailey, and for what apparent purpose, was next on the agenda for the Prosecution as a succession of witnesses were examined by Mr Young and his junior Mr O'Sullivan. First up was Jane Parsons, a photographer's assistant, who had lodged at Millbrook while Bailey and Kate, together with little Hollie, were also resident. She told the Court of a letter she'd received from the prisoner dated 3 September, about ten days after she'd left Bourne End to return to her home in London. It read:

Dear Miss Parsons,
Understanding that your business is photography, possibly in

connection with a chemist, we are plagued with several wasps'
nests in the walls of this house. I cannot obtain sufficient
cyanide potassium to kill them down here. I should be greatly
obliged if you could obtain 4 to 6 ounces for me. Two of us are
stung already. I will forward cost on receipt. Thanking you very
much. PS, Will you please register package to prevent accidents?

Had she heard anything about wasps when she was
living at Millbrook? Yes, said Miss Parsons, adding that
Kate had also mentioned at the time they'd been
troubled with them. In the event, she didn't obtain the
cyanide and wrote back to Bailey telling him sorry, but
the chemist 'wouldn't sell it to me to send through the
post, as we did not use it ourselves'. To which she
received another letter from Bailey, dated 10 September,
which read:

I have to thank you for the trouble taken in trying to fulfil
favour asked of you. I am indeed sorry that you were blown up
so, but I am surprised at the chemist in feigning ignorance of the
use that I wished to put it to. It is common practice with ants'
and wasps' nests, and infallible when injected by a syringe.
Thanking you again.

Harry Hancock, of Zimmerman and Co, and Harold
Smith, of the chemists Allen & Hanbury, related how
they had received letters from Bailey requiring everything from Devatol, a drug used to induce animals to breed,
to hydrocyanic acid and chloroform 'for vet use', the
prisoner wrote.

Mr Hancock was asked by Mr Johnston, 'Now, Devatol is
not a poison?'

'No,' he replied.

'Have you ever in any way advertised this drug as being a drug which, when administered to a woman, causes her resistance to the advances of a man to be less than before?'

'No.'

'Have you ever suggested it should be used on human beings?'

'No.'

'This drug is not supplied for human use?'

'Not in that form.' Then Hancock explained that as well as red Devatol for animals there were also little white Devatol tablets for human use, 'supplied only professionally, not to the public'.

As Defence Counsel had opened up this particular area of enquiry, Mr Young couldn't resist milking it. 'I take it that it [Devatol] is made up for animals and also for human use and that the drug is the same?'

'Yes, originally.'

'It has the same effect with animals as with human beings, only the quantities would be different?'

'Yes.'

'I notice you say on page 5 of the little book [a pamphlet supplied by Zimmerman and Co with Devatol entitled *How to Ensure Success in Breeding*] that it is an extract from the bark of a tree, and that it is generally used by African natives to restore normal breeding functions. Does that relate to human beings?'

'Yes.'

'It did originally then?'

'Yes.'

'Is it used by natives for human beings?'

'That I could not say.'

'Just look at the reference that it is suggested on the report of African travellers. Do you really think that means it was given to pigs and horses?'

'I suppose it would refer to human use in that case.'

In the event, neither Hancock nor Smith, both London-based, were able to supply Bailey with any of his various poisonous requirements. All he received was 'one tube of red Devatol tablets, full strength'.

Much closer to home, Stanley King, a chemist's assistant, working in his father's Marlow pharmacy business, was able to give a more graphic account of Bailey's alleged veterinary ambitions. He met the prisoner for the first time on 21 September in his shop. Bailey said he was a vet, and asked if he could be supplied with drugs as he was practising at Little Marlow. He then asked for a veterinary price list. Three days later, there was a letter from Bailey with a couple of lists of items he wanted, including stramonia, chloroform and hydrocyanic acid. The following day, he called to ask if his order was ready and, three days after that, on 28 September, the day before the alleged murder, he and Kate turned up in person at the chemist.

'What did he say about her?' asked Mr O'Sullivan.

'He said he brought her as a witness to prove that he wanted the drugs for veterinary purposes.'

'Did he say anything about poisoning dogs?'

'Yes.'

'Is it a necessary thing to show knowledge in order to get poisons?'

'Yes.'

'I think you asked him certain questions in order to test him as to what the hydrocyanic poison was for?'

'Yes.'

'What did he say?'

'He said it was [for] poisoning cats and dogs.'

'Did you read him some extracts from the Poisons Act?'

'Yes.'

'Did he satisfy you that he had knowledge of the subject?'

'Yes.'

Cross-examined by Mr Johnston, King said he had discussed with Bailey the fact the nearest vet was more than six miles away, at Maidenhead, and that he, King, complained people were always bringing their cats to him. And yes, Bailey – who told King that 'he was working up a vet practice in Little Marlow' – and his wife laughed together about the situation regarding cats. Re-examined by Mr Young, King agreed that Bailey seemed 'rather anxious to have the order filled'.

'Did you say anything special to him on the 28th in the afternoon and had you the order ready?'

'I said I had no Scheeles' prussic acid 4 per cent and I only had the weaker, which was 2 per cent.'

'What did he say?'

'He seemed very anxious to have a supply at once.'

That evening, King's errand boy Alfred Darby delivered a package to Barn Cottage with the various drugs and poisons as requested and asked Bailey to sign the official Poisons Book he'd brought with him, which the prisoner did before taking it next door to the Post Office for his signature to be witnessed by one of its occupants, Mrs Helen Hester. She was asked by Mr Young if she saw Kate on 29 September and replied she had, during the middle of the afternoon, and that she seemed cheerful at the time. And, as far as she knew, wasps had not been a particular problem.

If the Prosecution witnesses had up to this point merely

sketched out a fascinating landscape occupied by the principal figures in an unfolding drama, then the next was quite likely literally to flesh out more details as well as raise the stakes by several notches.

Enter Dr Bernard Spilsbury, Home Office pathologist, at 43, just two years before he'd be knighted for his services to forensic medicine, already in many eyes the expert's expert. A debonair figure usually kitted out, according to recent biographer Andrew Rose, in top hat, tails, buttonhole and spats, Spilsbury had, by 1921, become not just a Prosecution staple but also a bit of a media star who, over the previous ten years, had given key evidence in the high-profile trials of poisoners like Crippen and Seddon as well as the 'Brides in the Bath' killer George Joseph Smith. No decent murder trial of the day was complete without him and his confident testimony.

There was a palpable sense of excitement in Court as Mr Young asked, 'Are you Bernard Henry Spilsbury?'

'Yes.'

'You are a Bachelor of Medicine, and Bachelor of Surgery, Oxford?'

'Yes.'

'You are a special pathologist at St Bartholomew's Hospital?'

'Yes.'

'Are you employed a great deal by the Treasury [the Crown] in these cases?'

'I am.'

Dr Spilsbury, who'd first examined Kate's body on the day after it was discovered at Barn Cottage, was walked through the evidence he'd given at earlier hearings as he confirmed once again that all the symptoms indicated poisoning, he'd found no disease to account for death, and that she 'was advanced six months in pregnancy'. But once the business of poisons and their effect – Spilsbury's stock-in-trade, as it were – had undergone the first bout of Counsel crosstalk in Court, the eminent pathologist suddenly found himself being asked to contribute in an altogether different field of medicine as the Judge asked, 'I want to know whether Dr Spilsbury desires to be regarded as an expert upon mental questions and insanity for, if so, we must cross-examine on this point. You have one branch of knowledge, and does your experience cover any other branches?'

'No, I should not like to claim any special knowledge. I do not claim to have any knowledge of cases.'

Undeterred, Mr Johnston, seizing on His Lordship's point, asked, 'You hear great cases in which the insanity of people is raised and people claim to be insane?'

'I have not had as much opportunity for experience in this direction as the average general practitioner.'

'Have you had to give evidence?'

'Not expert evidence. I do not think it would be fair.'

'Fair to refuse it?'

'It would be merely hearsay evidence, after hearing the evidence of a mental expert.'

Apparently satisfied, Mr Johnston moved from the mind quickly back to the properties of stramonia and prussic acid before, without even seeming to miss a beat, diving back in with: 'Will you give an answer on the question of the sanity or insanity of a patient? You have heard the evidence given this morning by the prisoner's sister, Mrs Jennings?'

'Yes.'

'Will you assume for the purposes of this question that the prisoner has had sunstroke, and that he has three times attempted to commit suicide?'

'Yes.'

'That as a boy he was clever and more than ordinarily intelligent, but deficient in judgement, and that from the time of his being at school he has been regarded as queer?'

'Yes.'

'That he has had two serious falls from heights, and possibly injured his head; though I cannot tell you to what degree, but both his legs were injured and that he has had to support himself in his physical work by two steel supports, that he has been constantly striving relentlessly to better himself in various ways not only starting in business, first as a dairyman, and secondly by starting a dairy, and thirdly by starting this system of musical notation. You have heard all this evidence about him in Court today. I will ask you to take it from me that the system has been completed, and is considered a clever system.'

At which point, and presumably with Dr Spilsbury wondering quite where all this might be going, Counsel was interrupted by the Judge who noted, 'The substance of that has not been given in evidence.'

'The reason I am saying this,' continued Mr Johnston, 'is that I shall be giving evidence to this effect in Court. I may give evidence that this invention was a system on which a businessman might expect to be adopted.'

Again, the Judge interrupted, 'We have no evidence on this point yet. The question is one of sanity or insanity.'

With his eyes turned back to Dr Spilsbury, Mr Johnston soldiered on with one of the longest questions – more a kind of extended plea – in Christendom.

'You have the fact that he was constantly striving, that he wrote plays, that he had produced a system of notation, and that he also made a couple of inventions which he submitted to the War Office, one being a range finder. Then you heard that he has three times attempted to commit suicide and that he has been in an asylum for three months. You have been told that he has apparently always been devoted to his wife, who he is now charged with murdering. Assuming that you were told that this man did murder his wife, and were satisfied that he had done so, you must consider his mental state. You must consider that he has made no preparation for concealing the evidence of the murder, and that the murder itself was committed at a time when he would be possibly completing this system of musical notation in which he had shown such strong interest. Would these circumstances in themselves suggest anything to your mind as to the state of his mind at the time the murder was committed?'

'Yes, I think that about as far as I can say on the question you ask me is that he is a very highly strung individual.'

'Can you tell me if you have already formed that opinion?'

'I have not sufficient knowledge of him professionally.'

'Do you say he is a type liable to mental breakdown?'

'He is a type which might be subject to breakdown.'

'As far as you say, you think he is a man liable to a mental breakdown?'

'Yes, but I would like to qualify it by saying that, if he had a mental breakdown, the evidence of that breakdown would last for a considerable time if it would lead him to commit any very great offence.'

'If he believed that he was still in communication with his wife, would that be a delusion?'

'It might be regarded as a delusion.'

'If he was under the impression that he was receiving messages from his wife?'

'Yes.'

'If it was a fact that he believed this kind of delusion, would it of necessity follow such a breakdown, provided the delusion was still there?'

'Yes.'

The Judge then asked Dr Spilsbury, 'Assuming that he believed that he got a direct message from his wife, whilst he was in custody, it might be an indication of some delusional insanity?'

'It might be.'

'Assuming that he really believed that?'

'Yes, my lord. I do not think there is any other point I can give further help on insanity.'

And, as if sensing by now that his own witness had been perhaps a little too easily diverted down a path which might seriously confuse the issue, Mr Young decided to bring Dr Spilsbury back from a world of Defence hypotheticals by asking, or more accurately positioning, his own potentially damning and equally long-winded set of Prosecution what-ifs.

'Supposing you find a man who gradually acquires possession of poisons with a great deal of deliberation, and then supposing that he had plans for taking to his house a number of young ladies that made the absence of his wife most desirable, and that directly a complaint was made against him he rushes off by train to Swindon, where you find he tells untruths as to where his wife is, and first says she is in hospital for a premature confinement, and then says that she died at three o'clock in the morning, and when the police arrest him he tells them that if they had not been too smart for him he would have taken some poison himself, and described exactly what he had done in administering the poison to his wife … taking all this into consideration, would you form the opinion that at the time he administered this prussic acid to his wife, supposing he did so, he knew the nature of what he was doing?'

'Yes, most certainly, on these facts.'

'Would you also think he was capable of knowing that what he was doing was wrong?'

'I should say certainly.'

That wasn't, however, quite the end for the Crown's star witness. After the Home Office analyst, to whom Dr Spilsbury had originally given four sealed jars containing portions of Kate's viscera, completed his evidence, the dapper pathologist was recalled by Mr Johnston to comment on another hypothetical – this time related to the size and effect of a prussic-acid dose.

'Supposing a larger fatal dose of prussic acid was given, it would be fatal sooner than if a small dose was given?'

'Yes.'

'What would be the minimum time in which a patient would become unconscious after taking a dose of prussic acid?'

'It would necessarily vary.'

'Would you say a minute?'

'Certainly not.'

'But supposing a patient was given very much more than a grain, would you expect that patient would have any power to call out?'

'There might be time to utter a single cry.'

'A patient could not get up and go downstairs?'

'Oh, no.'

'A single cry.'

Was that in the Prosecution's mind when Counsel asked Mrs Eliza Hester, another denizen of the family living at the

Post Office next door to Barn Cottage, to recall a screeching noise she heard after midnight on the night Kate died? Mrs Hester, who'd seen Kate (with Hollie) that afternoon and who 'seemed quite well and happy', said she thought the sound was caused by owls.

'Do you think there was any element of a human voice in the noise?' the Judge then asked her.

'I did not,' she replied firmly.

With the light beginning quickly to die outside while the Court itself grew dimmer on an already cloudy afternoon that had experienced a flurry of snow earlier, the matter of Bailey's musical notation finally came properly under expert scrutiny with the evidence of Dr Samuel Bath. He boasted at least three sets of professional qualifications after his name as well as a sprinkling of university degrees and authorship of several musical works. Organist at the parish church in Marlow, Dr Bath had already delivered a crushing verdict on Bailey's system at the Magistrates' Court back in October and he didn't hold back this time round. 'I called it then a grotesque absurdity; I adhere to that … I should say it is of no value whatever.'

Dr Bath's expertise and vivid lack of equivocation – which, reportedly, caused the prisoner to smile for the first time since he'd been in the dock – couldn't prevent Bailey's ever game Counsel from at least trying to temper, if not partially undermine, the expert's dogmatic testimony as they parried on matters of sharps, flats and accidentals – or, as was the case here, the deliberate lack of them in Bailey's system. However, for Mr Johnston it seemed to be a losing battle, especially when, having finally induced the witness to surmise that Bailey might himself think the system was good and had a future – hardly a ringing endorsement – the Judge, who later made it plain he felt that this particular cross-examination had gone on far too long, chipped in with: 'Could it be used as a system?'

'No, my lord,' replied Dr Bath definitively. That, effectively, was that.

It was heading towards 6.00pm and the likelihood that the jury would not only be 'locked up' for a second night but also quite possibly the entire weekend, when the first of Bailey's advertisement respondents made her way to the witness box. The ad that had originally drawn her to Bailey was by now infamous: 'Young ladies, not under 16, must be over 5ft 6in, well built, full figure, or slim built … Applications from all classes entertained, as duties will be taught.'

In reply to his ad, Miss Gladys Millicent Edwards wrote to Bailey at Millbrook asking for 'particulars of work required', before following it up five days later with another note, this time requesting a meeting. The following day, she heard back from Bailey, who wrote: 'You do not state your appearance, but I can give you an interview on Sunday, 5 September any time between 3.30pm and 6.00pm if you are able to connect train service. Work is new musical system; building up staff according to material.'

They duly met and, according to Miss Edwards, Bailey said he was building up a new musical system which he was 'putting on the market and he wanted several young ladies to demonstrate with it'. The wage would be three guineas a week to start. She told him she could play the piano, but only 'very slightly'. He asked her if she'd prefer clerical or demonstration work. When she replied 'clerical', he apparently 'seemed rather keen that I should demonstrate'. Her appearance, it seems, was deemed suitable.

When, eventually, arrangements were made for her to start

working with him, which, it was explained to her, might involve sleepovers, Bailey had moved to Barn Cottage from where he'd written that she would meet 'others of the staff'. On 27 September, Miss Edwards arrived at the cottage where she met Miss Winifred Field, only for them to be told by the accused that he had to leave for town 'partly on business' and that they could have the day off. When the two young women returned the next morning, they were informed, this time by Kate, that her husband hadn't yet returned, so they left again.

The following morning, 29 September, they once more arrived at Barn Cottage to be greeted, finally, by Bailey who started explaining his system of music to them. A short time after that, Miss Lilian Marks arrived. When the instruction finished, around 12.30pm, Bailey told Miss Marks that she was to stay that night, and would be relieved the next morning by Miss Edwards, who did, indeed, return on 30 September with her suitcase ready to stay that night.

'Did you see the prisoner there?' asked Mr Young.

'Yes.'

'Did he seem well, and quite in his usual spirits?'

'Yes.'

'And cheerful?'

'Very.'

She and Miss Field, who was due to give evidence the next day, were given documents by Bailey to copy.

'While you were at work in the dining room, did you hear a child crying?'

'Yes.'

'Did he say anything about that?'

'He made some remark about her. He said her mother had been called away to Swindon and that she had been crying at the top of the stairs for her.'

'Did you ask about Miss Marks?'

'Yes.'

'What did he say about her?'

'He said she had gone out for an airing.'

Miss Edwards finished her work around lunchtime and was told to return at 8.00pm that evening. When she did, she found the house shut up and in darkness. So she went home.

With the tantalising prospect of evidence the following day, Saturday, from Lilian Marks, who would likely give details of her all-night ordeal at Barn Cottage, and the spectacle of Bailey himself quite literally fighting for his life, the Court adjourned at 6.10pm.

6

NO SUCH THING AS DELICACY: DAY THREE

On Saturday morning, well before the jury began to make its way from The Bull's Head Hotel, where it had remained following a short, head-clearing walk around the town and a second night enjoying Mr Gargini's hospitality under the careful supervision of the usher, a long queue was already forming outside the Courthouse.

'It is doubtful if ever in the history of judicature in Bucks, a jury has ever been called upon to listen to a more gruesome story,' drooled the local paper, and the public clearly couldn't wait to hear it in all its prurient detail, especially ahead of a day which would probably go a long way towards finally settling the fate of the Musical Milkman.

But before Bailey was due to give his own account of the events at Barn Cottage, and try perhaps to persuade the jury that he was mad, rather than an arch villain, there was still the no small matter of more potentially damning evidence from two of his 'Young Ladies'. Of those, the one who set most pulses racing was Miss Marks who, it may be recalled, had been named as the alleged victim in several grievous charges against Bailey on the original sheet when the Calendar of Prisoners was first published.

Winifred Field was, however, the day's first witness and she effectively corroborated everything that Gladys Edwards had told the Court the previous evening, including being present at Barn Cottage the morning after the murder was said to have taken place.

Mr Young asked her, 'How did he [Bailey] seem to be?'

'Quite cheerful,' replied the teenager, who still lived at home with her parents in Marlow.

'He did not seem in any sort of distress, like a man who had lost his wife suddenly?' Counsel continued.

'No,' said Miss Field.

The Judge asked her if she'd noticed 'a plaster or anything on his neck', and whether he had a cough.

'No' came her reply to both questions.

'He seemed sound in mind?' His Lordship then queried, curiously.

'Yes,' said Miss Field.

And so to Miss Marks.

'I am enclosing particulars re myself, age 20, height about 5ft 7in, well built, fair complexion,' was how Miss Lilian Pretoria Marks, a grocer's assistant, who lived with her parents in High Wycombe, had described herself in reply to Bailey's advertisement. After taking her place in the witness box, Miss Marks told Prosecuting Counsel and the Court about her first encounter with the prisoner at Millbrook on 6 September.

'Well, he just laid out before me a music system, and told

me he had several young ladies who were in communication with him over this musical notation. He did not give very full particulars that evening because I was hardly sure about the work, and said I would like to talk it over with my people.'

'Did he do anything with your hands?'

'He asked me to place my hands on the table.'

'He examined them?'

'Yes.'

'Did he ask you to stand up, so that he might examine you?'

'Yes, against the door.'

'He put you against the door?'

'Yes.'

'Your hat was on, I think?'

'Yes.'

'Did he ask you to take it off?'

'Yes.'

'Did he make any remarks at all?'

'He made a remark that I was a well-built girl, and did I think I was 5ft 7in.'

Miss Marks was given to understand that sleepovers for her and 'other pupils' would be part of the arrangement and, after subsequent correspondence between her and Bailey, a date was finally fixed for her to start on 29 September. When she arrived at Barn Cottage, the Misses Edwards and Field were already in situ and together they then had two hours' instruction from Bailey. She heard the accused ask the other two girls to return the following morning, while she was requested to come back that same evening at 7.00pm. When she returned, Bailey greeted her and also explained that 'two young ladies from Scotland had arrived' and 'that they were tired and had gone to bed'.

It was also shortly after 7.00pm she had heard, as prompted by Mr Young, a young child crying upstairs. Bailey told her that was little Hollie who was in the bedroom leading from hers, and he would attend to her. She then had supper alone with him after which he said he was going outside to await the arrival of another young lady from London. She went outside with him and they stood together for about three-quarters-of-an-hour on the lawn; it was a nice evening, but soon she made her excuses and said she wanted to go to bed. It was now around 9.00pm.

When she finally got into bed, she could hear Bailey walking up and down stairs and several times at the pump in the kitchen. He also called out to her that as the other expected pupil hadn't yet arrived he would stay up until 11.00pm, and that if Hollie cried again he would have to go through her [Miss Marks'] room to deal with her.

'What did you say to that?'

'I said, "Was it necessary?"'

About an hour-and-a-half after she'd gone to bed, she heard the latch move – there was no lock – and the door opened. In came Bailey, she said. He went straight through into the next bedroom before returning soon after. No, she hadn't heard Hollie cry, Miss Marks told Bailey, who said he had, before he then sat down in an armchair by the adjoining door. After about half an hour, Bailey then spoke again. 'He said,' Miss Marks told the Court, 'he had come with the intention of putting a question to me.'

'Did he say anything to you about whether you had been to sleep?'

'He asked me if I had been to sleep, and I said "No".'

'Did he say, "Why not?"'

'I do not remember.'

'What did he say next?'

'He asked me if I liked the cottage, and I said it was all very well but I didn't want to discuss it at that time of night.'

'Did he say anything more about the cottage?'

'He said, would I like to be mistress there?'

'What did you say to that?'

'I said I would rather not talk about it then.'

'Was anything said about a licence?'

'Yes.'

'What did he say?'

'He said, what would I say if he had already got a licence to be married on the following morning?'

'I do not want to go into any further details, but did he then try and get into your bed?'

'Yes.'

'How long did he stay there? All night?'

'He stayed in the bedroom until 8.00am the following morning.'

'He tried to get into your bed from time to time?'

'Yes.'

'And you refused to allow him?' the Judge interjected.

'Yes.'

Compared with these incendiary exchanges, Mr Young's next question seemed strangely anti-climactic. 'Next morning, I think, you breakfasted, did you not, with him?'

'Yes.'

In fact, this was merely a brief calm that continued with some comparatively gentle questioning from Mr Young before the storm finally began to break after Mr Johnston stood up to cross-examine. His intent – to try to undermine the weight, accuracy and gravity of her evidence – was obvious from the outset. Ominously, he opened with: 'Miss

Marks, I am afraid I shall have to ask a few questions, but I will make them as few as I can.' Clearly implying he thought Miss Marks would surely have been out of the door at the first opportunity after her all-night tribulations, Counsel's questions about their breakfasting together seemed weighted with incredulity. 'Did you actually go downstairs and lay the breakfast?'

'Yes.'

'How long do you think you were downstairs before he came down?'

'About half an hour.'

After breakfast, Miss Marks asked if she could go for a walk.

'Did he raise any objection?'

'No.' In fact, she added, he asked if she could buy some lunch while she was out.

When the Misses Fields and Edwards returned to Barn Cottage that morning, Miss Marks finally made her 'getaway' and walked 40 minutes to Cores End, the other side of Bourne End, where she went to the home of the Reverend John Allen, a Congregational Minister and old friend of the Marks family, to whom she told her story.

If Miss Marks thought this was to be the full extent of Counsel's 'few questions', she was sorely mistaken, for Mr Johnston was merely warming up as he now began to walk her minutely through the events of 29–30 September, from the moment she arrived back at Barn Cottage around 7.00pm. After a query about the time lapse between the events themselves and her official recollection of them in evidence given at the Magistrates' Court last October, after they were put down in writing just two or three days before the hearing itself, he asked, 'It is three-and-a-half months since this tragedy occurred?'

'Yes.'

'Could you at this time feel sure of the exact words that the prisoner used?'

'I cannot say.'

'What you do say honestly is that about 26 October, you put down what you could recollect and the impression the words had made on your mind?'

'Yes.'

'Naturally, you could conceive no motive but an improper motive for the prisoner coming in on you?'

'No other reason.'

'From his conversation with you, did it occur to you that the prisoner had a very good and reasonable motive for being in that room, and for preventing your calling the neighbours and making a disturbance?'

'No.'

'Perhaps any passionate desires that he had as regards yourself were shown to you, and caused you to form that impression by certain things he said?'

'No, I do not know.'

'Well, the prisoner has an explanation for his being in your room which is not the one which you most naturally thought.'

Then the Judge chipped in with: 'You cannot say that truthfully,' to which Mr Johnston replied, 'Quite so, but the prisoner is going to give one.'

That wasn't enough for His Lordship who asked Miss Marks, 'How does it happen that he tried to get into your bed constantly during the night, half a dozen times or more?'

'More.'

'He tried to keep you from going where you could call the neighbours?'

'Yes.'

Possibly rattled by the Judge's intervention, which seemed merely to abet Miss Marks' unswerving account, Mr Johnston tried a new tack as he turned again to the witness. 'I am not going to take you through everything that occurred that night. I prefer not to, as there are ladies on the jury.'

This cut absolutely no ice with the Judge who swiftly countered, 'Now that women have to take their share on a jury with men, they must take their share in a Court of Justice where there is no such thing as delicacy, if it interferes with the arrival at the truth. I am therefore quite sure that the ladies on the jury will understand that it is most important when they take their places on a jury … the only duty of a jury is to arrive at the truth and give a proper verdict.'

According to the *Daily Express*, the three women jurors 'nodded their acquiescence'.

That, at least, was the green light for Mr Johnston to cast off any earlier notions of 'delicacy' as he now tried to rattle Miss Marks, old beyond her years, with a series of more probing questions.

'Did he say something about how he was going to carry out his purpose?'

'Yes.'

'What did he say about that purpose?'

There was no answer from Miss Marks, so the Judge nudged her with: 'Just tell us what he said,' as Mr Johnston repeated, 'What did he say?'

'I cannot remember the exact words.'

'Just tell us the substance of what he said.'

'He said he had come with the intention of asking me to become his wife and, if not, pushing me into it.'

'He asked you some questions before then as to what you thought of the house?'

'Yes.'

'I put it to you that what he really said in the course of the conversation was this: "How would you like to be mistress of a house like this some day?"'

'Yes.'

'Might he not have said something like this: "You will be married yourself one day, and live in a house like this"?'

'He might have said this.'

Miss Marks said that whenever she tried to get out of the bed to go to the window and, indeed leave the room, he prevented her, pushing her back on to the bed; he did not leave her until daylight, she told the Court.

'Were these the only times he touched you?' the Judge asked.

'When he tried to get into my bed.'

'Do you say that when he tried to get into your bed you struggled hard to get to the window?'

'Yes.'

'You tried hard to get away?'

'Yes.'

'You gave a good account of yourself?' Mr Johnston asked.

'Yes.'

'The prisoner is not such a powerful man?'

'No.'

'As you struggled, naturally you were exhausted?'

'Yes.'

'You were exhausted two or three times during the night?'

'Yes.'

Now Mr Johnston played what might have seemed to be a crucial card. 'I am sorry to have to put to you one question … You have been examined by your family doctor?'

'Yes.'

'Your family doctor has told you that you are as pure a girl as you were when you went to this house?'

'Yes.'

'The prisoner did not have connection [an old-fashioned term for 'intercourse'] with you?'

'No.'

'You have already told me that you were lying exhausted on that bed so that you could hardly move three or four times?'

'Yes.'

'Was there anything to prevent this man from having connection with you if he wanted, when you were in that state?'

'No.'

'He did not have connection with you, and did not take advantage of you on that particular night. Is it not a curious thing that he did not?'

'No, he did not.'

'Do you not think you have made a mistake in what you have said to me about this?'

But, before Miss Marks could answer, His Lordship replied, apparently on her behalf, 'A young woman is not likely to forget what takes place on a night of this sort.'

It was a powerful, not to say deeply significant, intervention. It was the perfect opportunity for Mr Young now to grasp the nettle and exploit it. 'Fortunately, he did not have connection with you that night?'

'No.'

'Was that his fault, or was it your resistance that prevented it?'

'I fought hard all night.'

'Did you say he tried all he could to have connection with you?'

'Yes.'

'In the course of what he said to you that night, did he say anything about somebody being the mother of his children?'

'Yes.'

'What did he say?'

'He said he wanted me to be there, and make me the mother of his children.'

'Did he say something to you in the morning about suggesting you might not marry some other man?'

'Yes.'

'What did he say?'

'He said, did I think I was free to marry any other man, and I said, "Yes".'

'Did he mean after what happened in the room?' the Judge asked.

'Yes.'

'What did he say in answer to that?'

'He said I must know I was not, because something had passed from him to me which made it impossible for me to marry.'

'That was the view he took of what he had done that night?' Mr Young asked.

'Yes.'

Perhaps perceiving he was now on something of a losing wicket, Mr Johnston sought clarification. 'As regards this conversation when he wished to make you the mother of his children, is it not your recollection of it that he said he wanted you to be mother to his child?'

'No, he did not,' replied Miss Marks, still unfazed. 'He said he wanted me there to make me the mother of his children.'

'To be the mother?'

'Yes.'

'Did you regard it as looking after his child, or producing others?' said Mr Young.

'Producing others.'

And that was her final word on the matter.

If the public in Court had been electrified by Miss Marks' evidence, they must have been bordering on hysteria when they heard that the famous Dr Spilsbury was to be recalled next. In fact, the star scientist would be detained for just the briefest time as he explained about the application and effects of chloroform.

Then the recall of Inspector West, too, was merely to establish the discovery of a 'little green book' in a bedroom drawer – a book that would be 'put in' during the prisoner's evidence. This did lead, though, to a rather bizarre exchange at the conclusion of the police officer's stint after Mr Johnston had asked for 'articles of female apparel', under which the little book had been found, to be produced in Court. Inspector West did as requested, to which Mr Johnston declared, 'I put it to you that these are men's running shorts.'

The inspector replied, 'I should say they are a pair of women's bloomers.'

His Lordship ordered they be handed to the jury.

There was nothing so enigmatic about the evidence next of the Reverend Allen who, questioned by Mr O'Sullivan, told the Court that after he'd seen Lily Marks he visited Barn Cottage where he tried to get some answers out of Bailey.

'He asked me if I'd come specially to enquire about any special case as I'd mentioned young ladies to him. I said, "Yes, you had Miss Marks staying here the other night."'

'Did he seem to remember the name of Miss Marks?'

'No.'

'He seemed to know nothing of her?'

'No. He said, "Marks … Marks?"'

'What did you say then?'

'I said, "You must know the name very well … you have a list of the pupils you have been receiving." I suggested he might consult that, but he did not do so.'

'Did he say how many pupils he had?'

'I think he mentioned about 30.'

'Then what did you say to him?'

'As he persisted in feigning no knowledge of Miss Marks, I said, "We are only wasting time; perhaps you will be more ready to answer questions put to you by the police," and upon that I made to go.'

'What did he do then?'

'He then assumed a readiness to discuss things, and said, "Oh, Lily Marks." I said, "Don't be silly, how can you remember Lily Marks if you cannot remember the name of Marks at all?"'

'Then I think you left after making some remarks about Lily Marks?'

'I said, "Oh, well, any information you have had better be kept for those who will ask with more authority than I have."'

'Did the prisoner seem a little flurried?'

'He might have been.'

Apart from the recall of Zimmerman and Co's Mr Hancock who was required to confirm some detail about the dates of correspondence with the prisoner, the last major witness for the Prosecution was PC John Gray, based in Bourne End. He explained to the Court how, on instructions, he had kept an eye first on Millbrook then on Barn Cottage because of the frequency of young ladies visiting those premises. Two days before Kate's death, he said he'd seen Bailey and his wife walking together along Little Marlow Road.

'How did they seem?' Mr Young asked.

'They appeared to be very happy together,' PC Gray replied.

Just five days later, PC Gray found himself in charge of the prisoner at Marlow after Bailey had been arrested.

'Did he speak to you?'

'Yes.'

'Did you ask him any questions?'

'No.'

'Did you make a note of what he said within a minute or two afterwards?'

'Yes.'

'Will you tell me what he said?'

So PC Gray repeated to the Court what Bailey had told him in outline about the events of 29–30 September and which Gray had first told Magistrates back in October. Bailey's own official statement to the Magistrates was then read out by the Clerk for the record. That concluded the case for the Prosecution.

Because there is no proper record of Mr Johnston's opening remarks before presenting the case for the Defence, this, instead, is the *Bucks Free Press*'s account of Counsel's introduction; even in third-person reportage, it is clearly a thing of desperation, grasping at straws.

Immediately, Mr Johnston rose to address the Jury for the defence. He made a few remarks on behalf of the friendless man who had for nearly three days been sitting in the dock. He asked the Jury not to picture him as he now was – unshaven and bearing the stress and strain of his long wait in prison – but to picture him as the smart man he was known to be while in the Bourne End district discharging his duties.

If found guilty, it would be for the Jury to send him to his death, or to what might be described as a living death in a Criminal Asylum. It was abundantly clear that the prisoner had lived happily with his wife. He had a little daughter unprovided for, an aged mother, and brothers and sisters, who, if he were convicted, would be branded in a sense with the shame. He wanted them to remember that Bailey was a milk roundsman, with something like 300 customers. He was a man highly respected by those customers. He had striven hard to improve his position; of that there was no doubt. He implored the Jury that instead of coming to the conclusion that he was the greatest villain they had ever heard or seen, to decide that he was mad, and it was clear that he was mad in a sense.

The defence to the charge, he would at once say, was that the prisoner's was not the hand that administered the poison to his wife; that his was not the brain that conceived the idea of poisoning her; but that she committed suicide, as she had every temptation so to do, and they would hear that she had every possible motive. He would go further and say there was no evidence of any criminal assault on Miss Marks. Bailey went into her bedroom for a special purpose, for which the Jury would no doubt have an inkling. With regard to Miss Marks' evidence, Bailey would explain to them all the circumstances.

And so to the main event. Amid a flutter of excitement,

Bailey, looking even smaller than his 5ft 4½in, made his way slowly from the dock to the witness box where he sat down and gripped the side of the box in preparation for the inevitable barrage of questions from Counsel. From one of them, he faced the immensely experienced veteran for the Prosecution; his interests would be protected by a rather more callow Defence barrister. Both of these men were now about to be more focused than at any other time of the trial as, over the next five hours, they would effectively juggle with his life.

'Answer these questions quietly, and take your time about them,' Mr Johnston began sympathetically as he let his client fill in some of the — admittedly selective — history about his early life and times, including his father's premature death from acute melancholia and, more especially, his own medical misfortunes. These included sunstroke, ruptured knee ligaments (at a cider mill) and, later, another knee, together with a head injury (sustained while cleaning windows), not to mention mental breakdowns, attempts at suicide and a three-month stay in an asylum. In between all these ills, there was employment in farming, as a dairyman (in Cornwall) and as a milk roundsman in London for the Express Dairy Company.

This took us up to 1915 when Bailey was 27 and the Great War had been raging for more than a year. Bailey told the Court he had submitted two inventions to the War Office including one for sight-reading for aeroplanes. He said he made two attempts to enlist in the Army and was taken eventually 'but on the training ground my knees gave way'. After moving to London and marrying Kate on 12 August 1916, he toyed with various business opportunities before 'I broke down again'. Eventually, he and Kate, now parents of Hollie, moved to Millbrook in Bourne End where, when he wasn't working as a milk roundsman, he was trying to develop his musical notation.

'Things were going very well for you, then?' Mr Johnston asked.

'Very well indeed.'

'In every respect?'

'I was flourishing.'

'How were you as regards your wife?'

'On good terms, very good.'

'Did you love each other?'

'Yes.'

'There was no cause of disagreement between you?'

'Only the music.'

'There was the music?'

'Yes.'

'I must ask you to explain. Did you believe in it?'

'Absolutely.'

'Was it the enthusiasm of your life?'

'It was.'

'What was your idea of getting it known? Did it seem so very difficult?'

'It was as simple as ABC.'

The only way to spread the word about the system, he said, when prompted by Counsel, was to have it copied and as widely disseminated as possible. He asserted that the advertisements were not part of some plan 'simply to lure young girls' to his house.

'What was the future prospect of the scheme?'

'It was assured.'

'What was assured?'

'The thing itself … the money part of it. It was bound to be a success.'

'You thought eventually it would bring you money?'

'Absolutely.'

Mr Johnston then returned in some detail to the matter, which had been alluded to in just one brief exchange earlier – that of the serious divergence of opinion between husband and wife about the music.

'What did she think of your new idea? Did she persuade you to drop it at once?'

'Yes, she was afraid of it because of my health and the general foolishness of what I was doing.'

'Anything about your time?'

'Of course she complained I was not paying the attention to her I had previously been doing.'

'And spending all your time on the music?'

'Yes.'

'In August, did you make her any presents?'

'I was always buying her something.'

'In August, did you make her any special present?'

'I bought her a new costume.'

'Did you tell her about it?'

'No.'

'Was it to be a surprise?'

'Yes.'

'One day, did you send her a message about anything?'

'I asked her to come and meet me coming home from work, and she done so.' 'What was she wearing?'

'An old costume.'

'As she was not wearing the new costume, were you disappointed? Did you say anything about it?'

'I was displeased.'

'You told her so?'

'Yes.'

'Was this,' the Judge asked, 'after you gave her the new costume?'

'Yes, my lord.'

'What did you say?'

'I said she made herself look common.'

'Was that all you said?'

'Well … I walked away.'

'Why did she make herself look common?'

'Wearing a dress she had worn some time.'

The Judge then asked if it was shortly after this that Bailey found something in his wife's handwriting. Yes, he replied, the little green book that had been referred to by Inspector West earlier in the day, containing a purported note – the one first revealed at the inquest – from Kate to Bailey's mother. After the accused confirmed it was Kate's handwriting, the Clerk read it out to the Court with suitable gravity:

Mother, will you take care of little Hollie for me, or see she is taken care of: I can't stand it any longer – stand what you will want to know. I am not going to say anything: George can tell you all. I don't know if it is me to blame: It always is, so I expect it is me again. Never mind, it is nothing new: I wish my own mother were alive: it is a shame you are always called upon when anything goes wrong: it will be the last time where I am concerned. If I only knew Hollie would be looked after, I would not care a hang, and George would not mind if he never saw me again. I am all right to get his food for him, but otherwise I am common. Oh, mother, it hurts too much to be told that after what I have, what we both have, been through together. I am not so showy as I used to be: God knows I have had it all taken out of me: the shame, the disgrace of it all: can you wonder I feel quiet, want to dress quiet, want to keep away from everybody? I can't always forget, if George can.

When Bailey found the note, he said that he'd asked Kate 'what she meant by it'.

'You did not want your wife to commit suicide?' the Judge asked.

'I did not. I told her to forget the incident. I was only angry for a moment.' He added that she said, 'It was to bring me to my senses.'

His Lordship clearly had some theory of his own that he wished to pursue so he continued, 'This book has a considerable number of spare pages all blank right through?'

'Yes.'

'How came you to find this book? When did you find it?'

'A few days after the costume incident.'

'How came you to find it?'

'One day when I was upstairs at Millbrook, I should say.'

'Was it in a box?'

'It was on the chest of drawers.'

'Lying on the chest of drawers?'

'Lying on the chest of drawers.'

'In the room?'

'Yes.'

'Did you ask her to write anything of the sort?'

'No, my lord.'

'Did you ask her to write anything that might look dramatic in a play?'

'No.'

'Did you discuss plays with her?'

'Never.'

In an attempt to nip this diversion in the bud, Mr

Johnston weighed in with: 'How long is it since you wrote your last play?'

Bailey had mentioned he wrote poetry and plays when younger.

Bailey replied, 'Ten years.'

With a luncheon adjournment beckoning, the Judge pressed the prisoner on the matter of his marriage. 'No disputes at all?'

'No.'

'Quite happily down to the time when she died?'

'Yes.'

'Are you sure?'

'I will not say "quite happily", because of the business.'

'Were you happy with her?'

'I tried to make her happy.'

Anxious to try to clarify quickly the circumstances in which Bailey had discovered Kate's little green book, Mr Johnston asked, 'Did your wife say anything to you as to why she put the book on the chest of drawers, where you found it?'

'Yes.'

'Were you ever told why it was there?'

'She left it there for me to see.'

'How did you know she left it there for you to see?'

'I presumed it … she did not tell me.'

Following a 45-minute break, the Court reconvened at 3.00pm with Bailey once again gripping the sides of the witness box while, for the time being at least, still ever gently being probed by his Counsel. He was asked to recall his homes in Bourne End and Little Marlow and address the matter of wasps and ants and by what means he had wished to rid himself of both. Mr Johnston drew his attention to the fact that in correspondence Bailey had appeared to muddle them in terms of their actual location. The prisoner admitted he had indeed mixed them up.

On that subject and with regards to what Bailey had hoped might also be future money-making opportunities in farriery and veterinary work – such as destroying cats and dogs – Bailey claimed that many of the customers on his milk round asked him about undertaking such a service. The continuing question-and-answer then centred briefly on the prisoner's motives for the acquisition of drugs and dangerous poisons.

And so to the arrival of the various young ladies, but more specifically the events of the afternoon of 29 September after he'd asked them to leave before perhaps up to four might be returning later to sleep over that night. After lunch, he and Kate had spent some time together in the garden. When he came back into the house, into the dining room to be precise, Bailey said he could smell stramonia. How did he know the odour? his Counsel asked. Because of past experience, Bailey replied, when he had once 'attempted suicide'. What did Kate say when he asked her what she'd done? 'She said she had done it, or words to that effect.' She'd taken, said Bailey, 'roughly speaking, about a quarter of a bottleful'.

'What crossed your mind when you looked at the bottle?'

'The first thing that flashed across my mind was it was not sufficient to cause death.'

'How did it appear compared with the dose from which you recovered?'

'I could not tell you whether it was as much as I took.'

'Did you form any opinion as to whether your wife was likely to die or not from the amount that was gone?'

'I thought she would not die.'

With her legs, knees and arms shaking, Bailey told

the Judge he took Kate out into the garden 'to make her move about'.

'Did she say she wanted to die?'

'She did not. She simply said, "I have done it."'

'Did she want to die?'

'I would not let her.'

'How long did this walking backwards and forwards go on for?'

'Some considerable time.'

Bailey then told the Court he decided to take her back in the house because he thought she was recovering, and he made her have some tea and made her eat.

'What next?' Counsel asked.

'Then she complained of a nasty sensation at the back of her mouth, and I got her some lemonade.' Her condition, he told the Court, 'seemed to be improving'.

Once again, the Judge chipped in. 'Did you and she agree to commit suicide?'

'That was some time before.'

'When did you agree to commit suicide?'

'Three years before.'

'Before your marriage?'

'After our marriage.'

'How long after marriage?'

'Well, about 12 months.'

'How did you agree to destroy yourselves then?'

'By poison.'

'What poison?'

'There was nothing definitely settled on.'

'Was that before your baby was born or afterwards?'

'Before the baby was born.'

'Did you do so?'

'We did attempt to poison ourselves.'

'What with?'

'Opium and laudanum.'

'Did you each take it?'

'We did.' This attempt, said Bailey, took place at Winchester.

'Why did you agree to commit suicide?' was the Judge's obvious if rather belated question in this exchange.

'Everything seemed hopeless,' the prisoner replied.

Bailey then explained that, after he'd urged Kate to go to bed at around 6.30pm, he suddenly noticed in the dining room a stick of red sealing wax and, in the fender, the cap and string off a bottle of prussic acid. He rushed upstairs and saw Kate with an eggcup to her lips and, beside the bed, on a chair, the bottle itself. He went to Kate and took the eggcup from her as she was drinking the contents. She vomited and turned her head on one side; some of the vomit went on to the back of his coat causing a stain, he said, adding that as she fell back she uttered 'one or two words' which, as far as he could understand them, were 'Come too'.

Bailey was asked by the Judge to take his coat off and point to where the stain was so that the jury could also see it.

After hearing that his sister had drawn attention to the stain when Bailey had returned to Swindon and that he had succeeded in 'scraping it off, or most of it', Mr Johnston asked him, 'How long have you been wearing that coat since?'

'Only since I have been at these proceedings.'

'Have you been wearing an overcoat over it?'

'I have been wearing an overcoat.'

'How came the stain to be on your coat tail at the back?' the Judge enquired.

'I was by the side of the bed. When she turned her head

and vomited, some of the vomit went on the carpet behind and some went on my coat.'

'If you were facing the bed I cannot understand how the vomit got on to the back of your coat?'

'She turned her head towards my shoulder.'

Bailey then rushed downstairs, he told Counsel, to get some chloroform because he thought it would 'ease her pain'. He poured some on cotton wool and applied that to her nostrils for 'just half a second'. Kate was still alive and breathing heavily when he applied the chloroform, he said, but then died almost immediately. When her breathing stopped, his immediate thought was 'I was going myself', but when he saw 'the kiddie [Hollie] on the bed' he changed his mind, concerned that she would be left unprovided for.

At that moment, he also said he felt the need 'to conceal the fact' that his wife was dead because it 'flashed into my mind that everything seemed so against me'. This concealment continued with a vengeance when Lily Marks returned very soon after Kate had died. As they dined together downstairs, Kate was lying upstairs, her body covered apart from her face, with Hollie in bed next to her. That's how it remained until the following morning, when he moved Kate's body under the bed, covered with a sheet.

He admitted he'd told Miss Marks about the arrival earlier of two young ladies from Scotland 'to keep up appearances and allay suspicious thought of any sort'. He'd said they were tired and had gone to bed, and were not to be disturbed because he wanted to prevent Miss Marks from going into the room where she would have seen Kate's body. Yes, he'd gone to Miss Marks' room after she went to bed using the pretext that Hollie had cried – which he now agreed she had not – so he could sit in a chair by the door to the room where Kate was lying. He did talk to her on and off during the night but had, he assured Counsel, never a notion of 'injuring that girl morally'.

While contradicting her testimony about his supposed intentions towards her, Bailey did agree he had put his hand on her more than once to prevent her from getting out of bed and perhaps investigating the next-door room so causing 'a disturbance'. To keep her from the room, he did 'tell lies … all lies … just to conceal it'.

Changing tack dramatically, Mr Johnston next asked Bailey about the letter that was found in his pocket on Reading Station, which was addressed 'To the Coroner only (via the Police)'. The defendant said he had written it while waiting for over three hours at Paddington Station on his way back to Swindon.

'What did you write it for?' asked the Judge.

'Just to explain everything. Just to explain everything and take all the blame.'

'What blame?'

'As regards my wife's death.'

Mr Johnston resumed his questioning. 'In this document, you remember you said this: "I should like our three bodies laid together. That is why I came back to take one last look. Give one last kiss to my beloved. I gave her stramonia first, then hydrocyanic." How did you come to write this?'

'Well, I know I had broken my wife's heart.'

'How?'

'By keeping on with the music.'

'Broken her heart because of the music?' the Judge reiterated.

'Yes.'

'You said you wanted to take the blame. The blame of what?' asked Mr Johnston.

At this point, Bailey, who had been obviously tense in the

witness box yet still sufficiently self-possessed to counter everything thrown at him ahead of the biggest test of all – the Prosecution's cross-examination, which still lay ahead – completely broke down as he stuttered, 'The blame of everything.' This rare show of emotion had clearly ambushed his Counsel who hurriedly told the prisoner, 'Pull yourself together. This is very important. You have told us what you wrote is not true?'

'Yes,' said Bailey, slowly recovering his composure.

'Tell us why you wrote it?'

'I did not want them to know she had committed suicide.'

There was, it was noted by a court reporter, 'a deadly silence' in Court when Mr Young rose to begin perhaps the most pivotal phase of the trial, and he started as he intended to go on, in full confrontational mode. 'Now, Mr Bailey, you have given us a number of incidents in your life from the time you left school until the year 1920?'

'Yes.'

'You do not wish the jury to believe that this is a correct record of how you spent your life during that period. It is just a bare outline of certain incidents in your life?' 'Yes.'

'It is not a full account of all that you did and all the places that you visited?'

'No.'

While the jury at that moment had little opportunity to explore the details of Bailey's upbringing, or begin to piece together for themselves some of the factors that may have contributed to the psyche of the man sitting before them in the dock, it is perhaps illuminating for us to do just that. So, as the trial is placed temporarily on hold, it's worth examining the life and very peculiar times of George Arthur Bailey.

7

A VERY PECULIAR MAN

George Arthur Bailey – alias George Arthur Cox, alias Ronald Gilbert Tremayne (or Tremaine), alias Ronald Gilbert Treherne, the last three names having been acquired over 12 years of on-off petty crime before the tumultuous events of 1920 – was born in West Hampstead, north-west London on 13 March 1888, a month before Jack the Ripper began his three-year reign of terror in the East End of the capital.

He was the seventh of eight children born between 1873 and 1892 – his four brothers were Richard, Thomas Jr, William and Charles, and his sisters Mary, Emily and Helen – to Thomas and Betsy Bailey, née Hoyels (or Hoyles, according to George's marriage certificate).

Born and raised in Devon where he worked on the family farm run by his father Richard, Thomas Sr was 20 when, in

1872, he married Betsy, a fellow Devonian. The couple lived in south Wales before moving to West Hampstead where he worked for the Water Corporation, first as a general labourer, or 'navvy', before becoming a foreman. They moved into Lowfield Road, just below the brand-new Metropolitan & St Johns Wood Line, which opened in 1879. It was the third railway to appear in the district following the Hampstead Junction line from 1857 and the Midland in 1868, following the opening of St Pancras that year.

The Baileys lived at 9 Lowfield Road, possibly in one of the 42 new houses built there between 1877 and 1879. However, the next census, in 1891, now finds them on the other side of the tracks, as it were, albeit less than half a mile as the crow flies from Lowfield Road, at 115 Ravenshaw Street, a little terraced house backing on to the Midland Line, the northernmost of the three railways snaking through the area. That's the address given on George Bailey's birth certificate. But, just to confuse matters, it's also one and the same house in which an older brother, Thomas Jr, was living at the time of the trial – more than 30 years later – when it was officially listed as 37 Ravenshaw Street. The confusion is explained when it transpires that the street numbering system was changed in 1892.

George's principal education took place almost within spitting distance of the family home, just a few hundred yards away on the corner of Mill Lane and Broomsleigh Street; the latter – now known as Beckford School – was also the name of the second of three schools opened in the area by the School Board of London. The SBL, as it was commonly known, came into being after the passing of the Elementary Education Act in 1870 and was charged with providing schooling for London's poorest children.

Although education wouldn't be compulsory on a national level until 1880, the Board passed a by-law in 1871 that compelled parents to have their children schooled between the ages of 5 and 13. By the end of the 1880s – Broomsleigh Street opened in 1886 – the Board, responsible in its time for constructing over 400 schools across London, was providing school places for more than 350,000 children. When George first passed through its doors, he found himself in the company of no fewer than 1,381 fellow pupils. In addition to teaching the three 'Rs', the school could also boast, by 1895, a cookery and laundry centre as well as facilities for manual training.

By all accounts, George was a very bright lad, attaining the highest level – Standard VII – ahead of most other boys of his age, before eventually leaving Broomsleigh Street in 1901 at 13 shortly after the country had exchanged eras, from Victorian to Edwardian, with the accession, in January of that year, of a new monarch. He was also, you may recall from sister Helen's evidence on Day Two, 'musical from quite a boy', able to play various instruments by ear including the piano, banjo, zither and mandolin.

His first job was as an office boy at Lockhart's, the coal merchant in nearby Cricklewood, but it seems this employment may have been interrupted, then rather swiftly curtailed, by a severe case of sunstroke affecting his spine (according to the doctor who attended him) which caused George to be bed-ridden for a month. The meteorological records for the July and August of that year indeed indicate temperatures in London soaring on occasion to nearly 31°C. Eventually back on his feet, Bailey next found employment – and, remember, he was still only 14 at the time – as an outdoor-porter for the grocers, Lindsey Brothers, in West End Lane, even closer to home.

He was still working for Lindsey's three years later when his father died. Thomas Sr contracted a severe bout of 'flu towards the end of 1904 and a six-week illness then turned into what one of his sons, Thomas Jr, said was 'acute melancholia' or, in present-day speak, clinical depression.

Towards the end of February 1905, Thomas Jr called in the doctor and the local Relieving Office 'on account of his [father's] serious condition'. Before the creation of the welfare state, Relieving Officers were responsible for sorting out cash payments, where applicable, for the elderly, sick or unemployed, as well as issuing orders for admission to the workhouse.

Thomas Sr, who, it seems, had been subject to fits up to the age of 16, was admitted immediately to the Hampstead Workhouse Infirmary. According to Thomas Jr, his father's 'degree of insanity grew worse and it was decided to send him to Hanwell Asylum'. But, before he could be transferred to the facility in West London, Thomas Sr died on 26 February. 'Acute Melancholia' and 'Exhaustion' were certified as the official causes of death.

According to an unpublished account of his brother's behaviour given years later after the trial, Thomas Jr said that George had been with his father in the garden when the most serious seizure occurred. 'George was very much upset and had to be medically treated afterwards. My sister tells me that his hair stood on end.'

Three months later, George left his job in West Hampstead and followed his family's roots, first to Devon, working on farms in Farracombe and Lynton before heading for Leicester. Not for long, though, because, later that same year, he was back with his mother at the house in Ravenshaw Street and ill for three weeks, Betsy would later record, probably with his first nervous breakdown. It was, however, a sort of 'rupture', which apparently was the cause of his being rejected for Navy service in 1905.

Soon after this, he left West Hampstead again and wasn't heard of, by his mother at least, for almost five years, during which time George's life had begun crumbling with disastrous results.

His first conviction was on 10 June 1908 when, at Northampton, he was sentenced to 20 months' hard labour for forgery and fraud. By this time, he is also believed to have married, under the name of George Cox, in the same town, one Annie Harman, and it was while on honeymoon in Barnstaple, north Devon, that he was arrested. George was still serving his sentence in Wormwood Scrubs when Thomas Jr and his wife received the following letter from Annie, dated 10 October 1909:

Dear Mr and Mrs Bailey,
I have wrote a letter to George and told him I am in trouble [expecting a baby, not his] *and thought you might ask him to get away from me as I think it will be best for both of us as the young man will marry me and as George will be able to look after himself as it will take him all this time to get through himself and I think it will be only right that George should do what I want him as I have been through so much over it. Write and let me know what he means to do as I shall come and meet him out.*

I remain yours truly,

Annie

George was released from prison three weeks after this letter was sent but there is no record of any more contact with

Annie. Thomas, who would later write that George had committed the crime to help foster the image that he was 'a fabulously rich man ... and almost hoaxed all Northampton', met him outside the Scrubs and took his brother back to Ravenshaw Street where he stayed for several weeks before disappearing again from immediate family view.

It is also worth noting for future medical reference that a couple of months earlier, David Ford, a cousin of the Bailey family, had been admitted to the notorious Bethlem Royal Hospital – better known as Bedlam – in St George's Fields, Southwark, suffering from melancholia and delusions. After seven weeks' treatment, he was transferred to a convalescent home from which he was eventually discharged on 8 December as 'recovered'.

Thomas's reunion with his younger brother 15 months later was traumatic, to say the least, after he'd been instructed by his mother to go to an address on the other side of Hampstead. Arriving at 1 Constantine Road on 2 February 1911, he discovered that George had, the day before, attempted suicide by swallowing poison. The attending medic, a Dr Owstry, asked Thomas if he could make a search of the house. Thomas did so and eventually found an empty poison bottle as well as a long, rambling, often incoherent and truly bizarre letter, or statement of so-called explanation:

> I, George Arthur Bailey of West Hampstead, whose death you will hear of in the morning, sends you these poems [of which no record], also this rough draft of play [again, nothing more] for you to try and raise a little money for burial expenses etc and incidentally to see if they are worth publishing.
>
> Sir, I rely on your honour.
>
> Fate has given me more brains than enough, and a funny

nature. I have lived a life of deception and deceit. I have deliberately lived as I have done through curiosity to see what I could do; people have stood no chance against me; it will pay you to investigate my career if you want sensation and to see how I defraud people and yet, Sir, I am tender-hearted and hate the sight of suffering and have given my last penny away. I have suffered cruelly, my own fault. I have chosen someone to die with me [unexplained].

I am not frightened to die; there is nothing in death. I am sane but have seen enough of the world. The end of the world will be by the instrumentality of education. I can see it. I am an optimistic fatalist. Education will be the downfall of the human race. Why? Just ponder. Laugh at me now, but in 200 years time, I shall be proved right. There is more sin now, more restrictions placed on wrongdoing; education combats it and finds a way out. Is not life a hollow sham and hypocritical existence? The quicker we conquer our emotions and sentiment, the better it will be for us. I will say no more, perhaps the documents will explain themselves. All I will say is that all my life has been imposture, letters, forgeries and fables.

Do not blame my Mother or my Father. I was brought up in the right way but I deliberately transgressed it, and now my curiosity has killed me. Sympathise with my brothers and sisters, my friends and relatives, but not for me. I have enjoyed my life, have built around myself walls which I have had to destroy by the same means as I built them. I was told that my intellectual ability overbalanced my moral stability.

Perhaps so. I only advise other young men not to do as I have done. And please caution young ladies against young men. They are so foolish. Yes, Sir, I have wept over many a boy's and girl's downfall. Now analyse my nature. By the time you have read this, West Hampstead will be shocked by a

*double tragedy. My only regret is that people have no insight
with these things or with,*
   Yours truly
   GA Bailey
   PS I wish Jackson Clarke [no further information] *to
examine my knee. It has been horrible.*

Thomas handed over the bottle, subsequently discovered to
have contained aconite – often described as 'the queen of
poisons' – and the letter to Dr Owstry who then certified
George to be suffering from 'melancholia' and thus a suitable
patient for confinement in the infirmary at the nearby
workhouse. Indeed, this was the same Hampstead workhouse
where his father had died six years earlier. He was said to be
unemployed and destitute at this time and that his suicide
attempt was therefore partly attributed to this condition.

George was 'removed to' the Infirmary on 3 February and,
the next day, examined by the resident Medical Officer, Dr E
Claude Taylor, who concluded that the patient was 'a person
of unsound mind and a proper person to be taken charge of
and detained under care and treatment. The facts indicating
insanity observed by myself at the time of examination were
as follows: Depression – said he had failed to live up to his
ideal; said to have taken aconite and other drugs three days
previously so as "to end it all".'

Three days later, he went before a local Justice of the Peace,
Frederick Poynton Weaver, who, after hearing Dr Taylor's
diagnosis, made an order for George to be admitted to the
London County Mental Asylum at Banstead in Surrey, where
he arrived on 7 February. From the hospital records for
George, summarised by Dr Percy Spark, who was Medical
Superintendent at the time of his arrest in 1920, the new

patient was described as a 'gardener, married, 23 years of age. He was a case of melancholia, and ascribed his acutely depressed condition to loss of employment and family trouble, and admitted having taken aconite with a view to committing suicide. His condition soon cleared up and he was allowed to work in the garden. The patient admitted whilst an inmate of having been in prison for forgery at a post office, and he also claimed to have made an unhappy marriage but no name or address of wife, or record of any visit from her are recorded. The patient is said to have been a total abstainer.'

George was given a trial discharge from Banstead on 22 May and was then finally discharged a month after that on 19 June. At the end of July, he applied to the Hampstead Workhouse Infirmary for admission to the Farm Training Colony at Lingfield. These Colonies first came into being towards the end of the 19th century, mainly sponsored, at the start anyway, by the Salvation Army, whose founder, General William Booth, saw them as places for training 'the undereducated and underfed'. Every person in a Farm Colony would, said Booth, 'be taught the elementary lesson of obedience, and will be instructed in the needful arts of husbandry, or some other method of earning his bread'.

The scheme was also enthusiastically espoused by late Victorian Socialists such as George Lansbury and the Fabian Society founders, Sydney and Beatrice Webb, while the Colony at Lingfield, aimed principally at 'vagrants and paupers', was actually run under the auspices of the Christian Union of Social Service, a new offshoot of the Christian Student Movement which had sprung up in the UK at the turn of the 20th century.

However, for George, the pleasures or otherwise of Lingfield now suddenly had to wait because, on 11 August, an order was made for him to be admitted again to the Hampstead Workhouse Infirmary. On 5 September, he was discharged at his own request but then, the record states cryptically, 're-admitted the same evening'. A clue to this odd turn of events comes in an official statement – again from 1920, by which time the facility had become New End Hospital – in which the Infirmary's Medical Superintendent, Dr Arthur Reade, noted that, on 5 September, George went to discuss 'an invention of some kind' (sadly unspecified) with the House Surgeon, who refused to take the idea up. This, in Dr Reade's opinion, was 'evidence of unsound mind' – George's, that is, not the House Surgeon's.

Dr Reade also proffered the information that, on George's history sheet at the Infirmary, there was a record that in an application for relief he had stated 'he does not care if he lives or dies, and refuses his food; cannot sleep at night for the last three months; has altered brother's Post Office Bank Book from a balance of 4/2d to £299 and filled up a form for withdrawal'. There was also the more familiar intelligence about his prison term and an unhappy marriage.

Deluded, temporarily or otherwise, on the matter of his so-called invention, George was, however, found suitably sound of mind by 4 November to secure his requested transfer to Lingfield.

A couple of months after he was settled in Surrey, he may have heard the news that his cousin David Ford had had a recurrence of his own problems and was admitted to Croydon Mental Hospital, Upper Warlingham, suffering from melancholia and delusions. He would remain there until he died in January 1918.

After seven months at Lingfield, George relocated to Liskeard in Cornwall where he worked in a local dairy business for another nine months before his mental health once again took a hand and he had another nervous breakdown. Returning to live with his mother, who now had a house in Hampstead Garden Suburb, George found work as a milk roundsman for the Express Dairy Company, based at College Farm, Finchley.

And it is in Finchley where we hear of George's next brush with the law. On 13 June 1913, information was received at Finchley Police Station that George, who in the interim had made another suicide attempt using morphia, had embezzled various sums of money, and a warrant was issued for his arrest. Simultaneously, it appears that he had also absconded with a Miss Edith Denny, daughter of one of his mother's neighbours. Mr Denny told police he was fearful, quite reasonably, that George might kill his daughter and then commit suicide.

The couple were very quickly tracked down and George was arrested at the Beech Hill Café on St David's Hill outside Exeter and held pending the arrival of an officer from London to bring him back. Miss Denny was brought back by her father. The arresting officer reported that George had attempted to take a bottle of prussic acid from his pocket, saying, 'I was going to take that tonight. I was expecting this.'

The following month he was sentenced at Middlesex Sessions to six months with another six months of hard labour concurrent. At the trial, he handed the Judge a letter, which read, in the Bailey tradition:

To the Public: Please don't judge me; don't condemn me, don't pity me. Gifted and talented with numerous gifts and talents, I am yet a failure and have loved but once, and that is my darling Bessie. Kind-hearted and good-natured, I do most extraordinary things with criminal instincts and melancholic inebriation. You can guess how I have lived for four years: pain, energetic nature, the constitution of a horse and embittered by harsh and cruel misjudging. I have been a success and then with my own hands have helped destroy it. I wish to die.

The 'Bessie' referred to was Miss Bessie Hales, a book-keeper at College Farm with whom George was said to have 'kept company'.

For the first three weeks of his incarceration, George was kept under close observation by the prison Medical Officer who found him, according to police reports later, 'unstable and impulsive but saw no reason why he should be treated other than as an ordinary person'.

After his release, George's history becomes rather sketchy, although punctuated increasingly over the next four years, against the backcloth of the Great War, with minor offences, arrests and brief terms of imprisonment. His legitimate work, in the first part of 1914 at least, seems confined to the odd stint as a hospital attendant which went sour when he had a bad fall while cleaning windows and had to wear a support on his knee.

During 1915, George was twice in Court, firstly at Taunton for giving false information under the Aliens Restriction Act. The Act of 1914 was passed in the context of Britain being at war, and its provisions were principally aimed at controlling foreign 'enemy' aliens already settled in London, particularly Germans. It more specifically required foreign nationals to register with the police and allowed for their deportation.

In George's case, it appears he'd contravened the Act rather differently. On 3 September, he and a lady friend arrived at a restaurant in Station Road, Taunton, and asked if they could stay the night in one of its advertised lodging rooms. He signed in under the name Ronald Gilbert Tremaine, adding in the lady's name as his wife. Checking the new arrivals that Saturday, a local police officer, Sergeant Hart, spoke to George who gave him a card, which bore the name Tremaine. When Hart returned the next day, George admitted his name was Bailey, explaining that the reason for giving the false name was to protect the identity of his friend.

Three days later, George was up before the Magistrates pleading guilty to the charge of unlawfully giving false information. According to a report in the *Somerset County Gazette*, the Deputy Chief Constable, Mr Brown, told the Court that 'it was most essential under present conditions that everyone should give their correct names and addresses'. Chair of the Bench, Taunton's Mayor, Councillor Hinton, said the prisoner had 'pleaded guilty to a very serious offence and he had not committed it with his eyes shut. He knew perfectly well that he had done wrong.' George was sentenced to two months' hard labour.

A month later, at Devon Quarter Sessions, while still serving time, he got a further 10 months' hard labour under the alias of Ronald Gilbert Tremayne for having earlier stolen a pony, trap and harness at Paignton.

On release from prison in June 1916, and with conscription having been introduced that year, George, now 28, attested for the Army and was posted to the Devonshire Regiment, known as the 'Bloody 11th' after its participation in the Salamanca campaign during the 18th-century Peninsular War. At the trial, you will recall Bailey claimed he made two attempts to enlist in the Army and was eventually accepted, whereupon his knees 'gave way' on the training ground.

While he was still in training, halting or otherwise, his Regiment was in action on the Western Front, sustaining, like so many others, terrible losses on 1 July, the infamous first day of the Somme. Later that month, the Regiment distinguished itself at High Wood where Private Veale earned the Devonshire's second VC. Around this time, or soon after, George Bailey – Private 26991 – deserted.

It is not clear whether this latest shame had transpired by 12 August – the likelihood is that it had – for it is on this Saturday that, from records still available, Kate first and rather suddenly enters the story as George's 18-year-old bride at Lambeth Register Office in South London. Their marriage certificate, which mistakenly records George's age as '25' – was he 'bluffing' Kate from the start? – lists their residence at the time of marriage jointly as 202 Rommany Road, West Norwood. It was five miles south-east of Lambeth and far enough away from Devon to suggest George, now working as a dairyman – 'Milk Roundsman' was actually denoted on the marriage certificate – in nearby Streatham, might have been on the run at the time. There's also the distinct possibility that the marriage itself was bigamous since there appears to be no record of a divorce from, or dissolution of the union with, Annie Harman eight years earlier.

Many details of Kate's pre-history have, apart from the very barest facts, been almost impossible to track down. According to her birth certificate, she was born Kate Lilian Lowden on 19 December 1897, to John Henry Charles Lowden an 'Engine Driver (Stationary)' and Emma Augusta Lowden née Muff, who lived at 18 Carlton Street, Canning Town. Mrs Lowden made a mark – suggesting illiteracy – as the official 'informant' of Kate's birth when it was properly registered 'in the County of West Ham' the following February.

The next we know of Kate is contained on the marriage certificate where her rank or profession is listed as 'Cleaner, General Omnibus Company'. By this time, her father, now described oddly as a farmer, is also noted as 'deceased'. Her mother had died seven years earlier, in 1909, aged 50.

There is little else, apart from the record of at least one half-brother, a William Isaac Muff, son from a then 18-year-old Emma's first marriage to labourer Robert William Muff in the East End.

Prior to her association with George, which would, over the next two years, turn the couple into a kind of minor-league Bonnie and Clyde – albeit with the bride as a distinctly passive Bonnie – before a tragic end to her rather short and unhappy life, Kate had not at any time been, as the record had it, 'under the notice of the Police'. That was quickly to change.

In 1917, George was working first as a roundsman operating out of Milward's Farm near Lewes, Sussex, before, more ambitiously, attempting to set up his own milk and general dairy business in Farnborough, Hampshire. The plan was for Kate, in rented accommodation, to manage a tearoom and take in boarders. But, before the latter could come to fruition, George appears to have succumbed to another nervous breakdown.

Then, on 24 August 1917, accompanied by Kate, he stole from their lodgings in Torquay £11 10s in Treasury notes, a quantity of silver and coppers and a Post Office savings book, showing a deposit of £60, then absconded to London, finding lodgings at Brockley, near Lewisham. On 30 August, he stole jewellery and a chequebook belonging to their landlady, a Mrs Wheeler, before decamping this time to Eastleigh, on the south coast outside Southampton.

There, in the next phase of this pathetic crime spree, George, now using the alias Ronald Gilbert Treherne – the surname might have been appropriated from a rather fine neighbourhood house he would have known in his West Hampstead childhood – told local tradesmen that his and Kate's home in London had been destroyed by bombs in order to try to obtain goods and money by means of the stolen cheques. He claimed the cheques were from the insurance company in settlement for the damage.

He and Kate were quickly tracked down and arrested. On 13 November, at Hampshire Assizes, George was sentenced to three years' penal servitude for five cases of forgery and larceny; hapless Kate, in the name of Lilian Treherne, was indicted with her husband and given six months in the 'second division'.

There was, however, an extra complication. Just over a month before she was in Court to receive sentence, and while on remand like George in Winchester Prison, Kate had given birth to a baby daughter, Hollie, on 10 October in the prison infirmary. On her release early the following year, she and Hollie went to live in Swindon at the home of George's sister Helen and her husband James, and soon after that got a job nearby with The Cellular Clothing Company, pioneers of Aertex undergarments.

George, who had attempted suicide yet again shortly before Hollie was born, was some three months into his sentence at Parkhurst on the Isle of Wight when the Army, still preoccupied with the last terrible months of the Great War, finally caught up with him and he was discharged because of his imprisonment.

Eventually, in February 1920, having served two years and three months of his term, George was discharged from prison on licence and made his way to Swindon where he, Kate and Hollie would begin the final, fateful phase of their lives together that would come to a shocking conclusion in South Bucks less than eight months later.

8

IN THE LINE OF FIRE:
DAY THREE CONTINUED

B ack at the trial in Aylesbury, the jury were unaware of the details of Bailey's shady past – the rules of evidence prevented that – but Mr Young had subtly suggested the possibility of a chequered history. Mr Young naturally remained in full combative mode as he questioned the accused about claims of his and Kate's previous attempts at suicide. He insisted, 'When you were in any serious difficulty, your recourse was to poison. Is that what you suggest?'

Bailey said he didn't suggest that specifically but had, he agreed, done so two or three times.

'I understand that on one occasion you both took something, didn't you?'

'Yes. We were carrying them [poisons] with us.'

'Did you take them?'

'Yes.'

'When they were produced, did you say to her, "Now, swallow yours"?'

'No.'

'Just tell me what was done.'

'What she was carrying was for herself, and what I was carrying was for myself.'

'What happened?'

'You will have to give me time to think.'

'Did you not tell her to take the poison, and then you would swallow yours?'

'No.'

'What I am suggesting is, and I hope it may help your memory, that you prepared the poisons and gave her one, saying, "Here take that, and I'll take mine"?'

'I did not say anything like that. I would rather not say anything about it.'

'I want to know what actually happened on that previous occasion.'

'We drank it simultaneously.'

'I suggest you gave it her.'

'No.'

'Was your wife very ill after that occasion, after she had taken this poison?'

'Yes.'

'Worse than you were?'

'I am not in a position to tell you. I am not in a position to know.'

'But you both recovered?'

'Yes.'

Bailey told the Court that his music, about which he was, as Mr Young suggested, 'very earnest', was, in the weeks leading up to Kate's death, the sole cause of disagreement

Above left: The accused, George Arthur Bailey. ©*Daily Mirror*

Above right: George Bailey's wife and victim, Kate Bailey.

©*National Archives*

Below: The scene of the crime. A postcard from the early 1920s featuring Barn Cottage, Little Marlow next door to the Post Office. ©*Ken Townsend*

Above left: Bailey in custody. ©*Daily Mirror*

Above right: Happier times before tragedy struck. Kate and a two-year-old Hollie. ©*National Archives*

Below: Bailey gets off the train at a crowded Bourne End station en route to a police court in Marlow. Kate (inset). ©*Daily Mirror*

An example of Bailey's musical notation. It shows a comparison between the established system and Bailey's own method. ©*National Archives*

Above left: Samuel Sinclair Johnston for the defence, pictured at university.

©*Trinity College, Oxford*

Above right: Key prosecution witness Lily Marks. ©*Daily Mirror*

Below left: Mr Justice McCardie 'The Bachelor Judge', as dubbed by the Press. ©*Solo Syndication*

Below right: Hugo Young KC for the prosecution. ©*Nottingham Post*

Above: Dr, later Sir, Bernard Spilsbury, legendary Home Office pathologist.
©*Getty Images*

Below: Making legal history. Miss Tack, Miss Stevenson and Miss White
the three women jurors. Jury usher Mrs Noble (inset). ©*Daily Mail*

THE CHIEF'S LAST CHARGE.

The New Viceroy of India (to the New Juror). "MADAM, I COULD NOT LEAVE THE CAUSE OF JUSTICE IN FAIRER HANDS."

Punch magazine comments in January 1921 on the new phenomenon of women jurors.

©*Punch Archive*

Above left: Prolific hangman John Ellis.   ©*Solo Syndication*

Above right: A trial exhibit: an extract from the book of poisons – Bailey's signature clearly visible.   ©*National Archives*

Below: Oxford Prison. Bailey was remanded here and later hanged.

©*Oxfordshire Record Office*

Above: Hollie visits Old Barn Cottage in 1984. ©*Bucks Free Pres.*

Below left: Hollie at the site of her mother's unmarked grave in Little Marlow Cemetery. ©*Bucks Free Pres*

Below right: Author, Quentin Falk, researching the dark past of Old Barn Cottage. In the dock at Aylesbury Crown Court, one-time Bucks Assizes, refurbished to its former glory following a devastating fire in 1970.

©*Richard Tedhar*

between the couple. For his wife, 'it was causing many an unhappy moment', and it meant he was 'not attending to her properly'. She was, insisted Bailey, 'interested in the music but did not like the way I was going about it'. She especially didn't like the idea of his having the girls round the house.

'Did she protest?'

'She did not like the idea, but she would not quarrel over it.'

'You felt that she was a stumbling block in your way?'

'No. But she was not a help-mate.'

Yes, Kate was concerned at the financial implications of his continuing with the music and paying the girls but he claimed she thought, once the ball was rolling, 'it would be all right'.

'Were these questions of finance a constant subject of discussion between you and your wife?' Mr Young asked.

'Yes,' said Bailey.

Mr Young next came to the matter of Kate's tragic-sounding note to Bailey's mother found in the little green book. Had the prisoner ever mentioned the possibility of suicide when he was arrested or had he in any Court said, until today, he'd seen the note before the police found it? No, to both questions.

'It was produced at the inquest, and I suggest that until it was produced at the inquest you had never seen that letter?'

'I had seen it.'

'And you never said so until today to anybody?'

'That is wrong. I have not mentioned it to the outside world at all.'

'Now this letter is out, you suggest that your wife had threatened to commit suicide. Do you agree that this letter shows that she was on very bad terms with you?'

'She was not on bad terms with me.'

The Prosecution then proceeded to take Bailey almost line by line through the agonised note asking for his explanation or interpretation of Kate's sometimes cryptic lines. What was it, for example, she 'could stand no longer'? Bailey could make no suggestion. What was she to 'blame' for, and what could 'George tell you'? Those were merely references to 'the dress incident' and that, added Bailey, 'she was all for dressing quietly, and perhaps not dressing as I should like her to'.

'You liked something younger?' suggested the Judge, in a move presumably to provoke.

'Younger than my wife, who was 23?' replied the prisoner, refusing to take the bait.

'Your advertisement was for girls of 16?' the Judge persisted.

'I wanted young girls to explain the system,' stated Bailey blandly.

How, though, did Bailey answer Kate's pained charge that he found his wife 'common', which seems to have been for her the most wounding accusation?

'May I explain I meant common in appearance … I was continually buying her things to get her out of herself, and make her look better and dress well. I asked her to meet me coming from work, and she did so but came dressed in an old costume. I was displeased with it and told her she made herself look common, and then I walked away.'

'Did you think it was rather insulting to say to your wife that she looked common?'

'We were man and wife. We understood one another. I did not mean common; I meant common in appearance.'

Like a dog with a bone, Mr Young persisted in trying to get some kind of rise out of Bailey, who resisted as steadfastly, saying that he thought the purpose of the letter was simply to 'bring me to my senses'.

But that was still not good enough for Counsel who asked, 'Do you think she would have written things like this merely to "bring you to your senses"?'

'Did you know my wife?' Suddenly, an untypical flash of annoyance from the prisoner.

'No. You are not answering my question.'

'No, I did not.'

'I put it to you that in view of the disagreement between you and your wife, had you ever conceived the idea of poisoning her alone, or poisoning her and yourself?'

'I did not know there was any such arrangement.'

Mr Young moved on sharply to the matter of the young ladies and their proposed sleepovers at Barn Cottage. 'Do you think it would have been a nice thing to have attempted an attack upon the virtue of a girl when your wife was sleeping in the house?'

'No.'

'I understand you say it would not be the right thing?'

Bailey agreed.

'But supposing you had conceived such a wicked idea as getting a girl alone in the house, and going to her room for a wicked purpose, it would have been rather awkward if your wife had been in the house?'

'I cannot see I can answer that. I think I said my wife was sleeping there.'

'Supposing you knew it was desirable not to have your wife on the premises?'

'I cannot put myself in a position anything like that.'

Why would he lie to Miss Marks about the arrival earlier of 'two young ladies from Scotland', or tell her that the baby was his sister's child or lead her to think that he was unmarried if it was not to make her potentially more vulnerable to his 'lustful designs'? Why did Bailey seem anxious to get hold of poisons so quickly and, if he had the many customers he claimed wanting him to destroy cats and dogs, could the prisoner name even just one?

In the event, Bailey could only name one, a Mrs Collins, whom he said had asked him about dealing with a cat back in July. Why had he written to several chemists asking for prussic acid, requiring delivery in a particular week? Why did he require two forms of Devatol, and why was there evidence of it dissolved and handy in a meat-juice bottle?

To all Mr Young's fiercely provocative questions, Bailey continued to answer calmly and non-committally, except to emphasise that all drugs and poisons had been accumulated solely for the purpose of his proposed farriery business. But, pressed Mr Young, 'If you had got the idea of poisoning your wife on 29 September, you had got the means at your disposal?'

Yes, agreed the prisoner, 'the means at my disposal *if* I had had the idea.'

Mr Young then moved Bailey on to Exhibit 48, his letter to the Coroner. 'When you wrote that letter, did you think it would be read when you were dead?'

'Yes.'

'Did you also form the intention to make away with your child [Hollie] before you killed yourself?'

'It had been in my mind.'

'When you wrote that letter you intended it to be read when you, your wife and child were dead. Can you explain that letter?'

'I have been trying to explain it, and to a certain extent I cannot explain it because I left the kid at Swindon.'

'I am asking you, when you wrote this letter it was with the intention that it should be read when you, your wife and child were dead?'

'Yes. That was in my mind.'

'What object could you have under circumstances like this of putting into this letter a pack of lies?'

Bailey thought about this for a moment before answering, devastatingly, 'Because I would rather tell a pack of lies than the truth.'

'Why?' asked Mr Young, who must have been more than a little unsettled by the prisoner's unexpected response.

'I wanted to take all the blame.'

'Why should you take it?'

'Because I deserved the blame.'

'If you thought you were accused of the murder of your wife, why did you not say she took away her life?'

'I was morally the cause.'

'On account of your treatment?'

'On account of my treatment, things were not quite as they ought to be.'

Contrary to what was stated in the letter, he did not, he asserted, hand Kate the poison. He claimed that the phrases 'she believed my statements' and 'they are our secrets' referred to conversations that they had had previously about the afterlife. Or, to be more accurate, 'the future life', as Bailey called it. They had apparently discussed and agreed that their future together in the afterlife was assured. That was the only 'secret', he said.

Mr Young ploughed on. 'The letter then states: "I heard my darling die on Wednesday, 29 September at 7.15pm. I have waited my fate and now I meet it." Then later you say, "I should like our three bodies laid together. That is why I come back, to take one last look. Give one last kiss to my beloved." After you left on 30 September, did you ever go back to Barn Cottage?'

'I did not go back to the cottage.'

'Were you intending to do so before you committed suicide, as indicated in this letter?'

'I was intending to go back.'

'Then you say, "I gave her stramonium first, then hydrocyanic. No blame attaches to the chemist. I could always bluff to attain my ends." Your bluff was telling the chemist you were a vet?'

'That was simply to get the chemist out of any awkwardness, perhaps.'

'Your bluff meant when you wrote that letter that you had got the poison by pretending to be a vet?' the Judge asked.

'Well, I had it in my mind that it would be an excuse for the chemist. That is the only way I thought of.'

This was simply too much for Mr Young who asked his next question overlaid with a very thick layer of sarcasm. 'In fact, you were so magnanimous that, in order to shield your wife from the suspicion of suicide, you were willing to take upon yourself the character of a murderer, and you also told a lie as you were anxious to relieve the chemist from any blame in supplying you?'

'Certainly,' Bailey replied blithely.

'That was very noble indeed!' Mr Young continued, in the same vein.

'Yes,' said Bailey, steering well clear of the challenge.

As for his 'casual' conversation with PC Gray, not in any way an official 'statement', as had been suggested by the Prosecution, Bailey said he was simply 'trying to mislead him about the whole thing', and that he never made any suggestion to Gray, or to any other policeman for that matter, that Kate had committed suicide. When she did take the stramonia Bailey said he thought he did all he could to save her. No, he didn't call the doctor, nor the parish nurse who lived nearby, because he didn't want them to know that she had attempted suicide. Bringing them in would have revealed the fact, he averred. Later, when he made tea, she complained to him there was something burning at the back of her throat, but not that there was, as the Prosecution alleged she might have said, 'a bitter taste'.

At this latest dramatic juncture towards the end of the afternoon on a day full of twists and turns, Mr Justice McCardie halted the proceedings to enquire of the Counsel whether they thought the trial could be concluded that day or whether justice would be better served by planning ahead for a resumption on Monday – which would, of course, necessitate keeping the jury locked up for two more nights, as the next day, a Sunday, would be a rest day. The latter course was agreed without demur so the Judge ordered a brief tea break.

A little over ten minutes later, Mr Young and the accused resumed their sparring with Bailey claiming that Kate died almost at exactly the same moment Miss Marks returned that evening to Barn Cottage, and not much earlier as Counsel now suggested. Why, Mr Young asked, did he leave Hollie in bed with her dead mother?

Bailey didn't have an answer.

'Did you intend at any time to poison the child?' the Judge asked.

'I don't think I did.'

'You did not consider it?'

'Afterwards, of course.'

143

'When?'

'When I went to Swindon. It entered my mind then.'

Mr Young then said, 'Miss Marks has told us that the child was in the room next to her. Now, it is a horrible thing if you left the child in bed with the dead mother. I am pressing that point in support of my suggestion that, before Miss Marks came, you had hidden the body under the camp bedstead in No 4?'

'No.'

'Did you give the child opium to keep it quiet?' enquired the Judge.

'No.'

'Nothing at all?'

'No.'

'You have told us that this tragedy happened just before Miss Marks came. Why did you not say to her at once that your wife had committed suicide, but you told us that you received Miss Marks with a smiling face?' Mr Young asked.

'I said I did. I would not answer for anything I done.'

'Were you regretting your wife's death?'

'I expect so.'

'*Were* you?' Mr Young again asked.

'Yes.'

Bailey next denied each and every one of Miss Marks' claims about what he was supposed to have said to her during the course of the night – from obtaining a licence to marry and be the 'mother of his children' to becoming 'mistress of the cottage'. He had made, he insisted, no attacks on 'her virtue' nor did he ever suggest that she'd be in no position to marry any other man.

'Did you hear her swear that you gave her a reason, which I won't repeat, why she was not free?'

'Yes, I heard her.'

'Was that statement of hers true or false?'

'I will say it is false.'

'Do you dare to suggest that the young girl here wickedly invented the statement of what occurred?'

'I do not suggest anything, but I know it is wrong.'

Why, Mr Young asked, had Bailey at first denied knowing whom Miss Marks was when Reverend Allen came to the cottage?

The prisoner had no sensible answer for this, but he was clearer on the matter of why he wanted to catch a train that afternoon. No, not to escape, but to 'take the kiddie to my sister'. He agreed he did tell 'all lies' at Swindon, including one that Kate had been taken into hospital at Wycombe 'on account of a premature confinement'. He also lied to Mr Hall about being ill, and that he'd got 'something the matter' with his lungs. Why did he lie about this?

'Perhaps because I was going wrong,' Bailey replied enigmatically. He had held on to the prussic-acid bottle, and carefully sealed up the top, after Kate had taken it – but not been given it by him, he emphasised – with the idea he might poison himself. And, yes, the notion of also killing Hollie was 'in my mind all the time'.

Why, Mr Young asked, did Bailey put in his advertisement: 'Young ladies – not under 16'?

'I did not want too-young ladies; I did not want girls.'

'You knew more than that. You know the dividing line of 16 as to young girls?'

'What dividing line do you mean?'

'That it is an offence having connection with a girl under 16. Have you never heard of it?'

'Never.'

'Why ask particularly over 16?'

'I didn't want young girls with no knowledge.'

Why, the Judge then asked, did he specify 'full figure or slim build'?

'I wanted attractive persons, unique. It was a unique system. I wanted everything original.'

'You did not want anything common?'

'I did not want anything common.'

'Your wife was common?'

'In dress.'

'You did not regard Miss Marks as being common?' Mr Young asked.

'Miss Marks had got originality, what I wanted.'

Following the Prosecution's long and probing interrogation, which still wasn't quite at an end, Mr Johnston felt the need to dive back into the fray to try to get his client to clarify some of the preceding points, beginning with the age question. Re-examining Bailey, he asked, or rather prompted, 'You were going to teach your system to children, and it would not have been done to send round as teachers people under 16, as they would have not been responsible?'

The prisoner naturally agreed.

The Judge, however, wasn't going to let Bailey off the hook, quickly interrupting Mr Johnston's flow by querying just how the prisoner believed he was going to be able to pay these young ladies – the six he'd engaged – at three guineas a week. Bailey admitted he had not faced the prospect properly and because of his 'obsession' with the system he had simply 'not thought it out'.

Again guided by his Counsel, Bailey explained that, although he lied about his lungs to Mr Hall – with whom he was, he said, anxious to keep his job – he was genuinely not feeling well, having worked long hours, all night sometimes, on his music.

'After these long hours, what was the state of your health just at this period?'

'I was done up.'

'Physically or mentally?'

'Physically *and* mentally.'

Mr Johnston was also anxious to return Bailey to the matter of Exhibit 48 and, in particular, to two lines: '"My own dear wife knows and knew but she is so brave, so staunch." Why did you say that?'

'Because she knew what was going to happen. She could see how I was, and that there was another collapse coming.'

'If this document is right,' the Judge intervened, 'your wife died from poison that you gave her. Why did you say, "My own dear wife knows and knew but she is so brave and so staunch?" Did you mean your wife was still alive? Have you any explanation to give? It is as if you were in touch with her?'

To which Bailey responded, in yet another unexpected diversion, 'Of course, I believe in spiritualism.'

'Do you believe we can communicate with spirits in the other world?'

'We do not seem parted, but I cannot quite explain … I realise her presence at times.'

'Has she ever influenced your conduct since she died?'

'Yes.'

'Tell us about that?' Mr Johnston resumed.

'She did not want me to go to Little Marlow.'

'What do you mean?'

'I should not be here if she had not influenced me.'

'Do you think she is influencing your movements?'

'Yes.'

All of which was now rattling Mr Young who asked the Court how any of this had arisen out of his cross-examination. Undeterred, Mr Johnston carried on. 'You say in the letter, "Please that God will forgive her." What should God forgive her for?'

'Suicide, I suppose.'

Bailey's five-hour ordeal finally concluded with a series of questions from the Judge.

'You say you decided to conceal the death of your wife?'

'Yes.'

'Was that in order to save her name or save your name?'

'I think the real purpose was to straighten things out, and then follow.'

'What do you mean by "straighten things out"?'

'Things to be considered as regards our property, for instance, and then perhaps, finish it. That is the only explanation I can give: go away as I was without fuss.'

'When did you intend to kill yourself?'

'I suppose as soon as I had finished. I could not give a definite time.'

The Judge repeated the question.

'When I had completed my arrangements. There was the baby to think of. I did not know what to do.'

'You could not kill yourself?'

'There was the baby to think of.'

'You wished to leave things in order. You have already in your evidence told us that you made up your mind sometimes that you would commit suicide, and sometimes you said that you would try and work for the child?'

'Yes.'

'I do not understand what you wrote in this paper, but at any rate you were undecided?'

'Sometimes it was one way, and sometimes the other.'

On that typically ambiguous response, Bailey exhaled an audible sigh of relief as he left the witness box and returned to the dock. The *Bucks Free Press* offered a fascinating piece of 'colour' that wasn't included in the official transcript. During his cross-examination, Mr Young had at one point dramatically held out a bottle of prussic acid. As Bailey inexplicably stretched his hand to receive it, Mr Young said, 'Oh, no … I cannot take responsibility of handing it to the prisoner.'

It was now after 6.00pm and 'the jurymen looked tired', reported the *Daily Express*, 'but their three women colleagues appeared alert, one of them frequently taking notes'. In terms of sheer theatre, the rest of the day's proceedings were bound to be something of an anti-climax following Bailey's evidence, which had fluctuated wildly between the mundane and the sensational.

Mrs Baker and Mrs Rouse, mothers of two of the young ladies, Violet and Ethel – old school friends – who'd replied to the advertisements, confirmed that neither of their girls, who lived locally, actually turned up to their appointments. Both confirmed to the Court that their daughters were 'tall, good-looking girls'. A third girl, Mabel Tubb, from near Guildford, had two interviews with Bailey at Millbrook and they agreed she should come to Barn Cottage on 27 September and stay three nights. When Miss Tubb arrived, she was greeted at the door by a woman who told her Bailey had been called away. Yes, she thought it was Mrs Bailey she saw. No, she didn't go back again.

Before a halt was finally called at the extraordinarily late hour of 6.50pm, there was still time for one more witness, Bailey's brother, Thomas, ten years his senior. He confirmed his sibling had got sunstroke in 1900, which had made him ill 'for a length of time'. Had he been normal, or different from other people, Mr Johnston asked him. 'He was practically normal, but very erratic,' Thomas replied.

'We were told,' queried the Judge, 'that he was all right apparently as a boy, and then began queer conduct?'

'It was when he attempted suicide [and Thomas confirmed his younger brother's confinement to Banstead Asylum after one attempt in 1911] that my suspicions were first aroused.' As far as he knew, Bailey hadn't been committed to an asylum since.

The Court then rose, with the prospect of a quiet Sunday ahead, a day on which the Jury were granted permission by the Judge to attend church as long as they did so all together, before the trial would more than likely reach its dramatic conclusion on Monday.

9

THE FINAL ACT:
DAY FOUR

'The crowd, lined up in a queue outside the Assize Court, could only be likened to one usually seen outside a Picture Palace or a Theatre, instead of a Court of Justice, wherein the chief actor was fighting for his life. Once or twice the crowd rushed the doors and literally fought their way in, not caring so long as they could gain admission into the building.'

It was into this feverish atmosphere, as described above in the weekly *Bucks Free Press* four days after the trial ended, that the principal players filed for almost the final time. It was 10.30am on Monday, the jury having spent their day of rest attending Morning Service at nearby St Mary's Church, followed by a drive in the afternoon round the district in a brake pulled by a pair of horses.

As the Judge took his seat, Bailey entered the dock. He

bore, said observers, 'unmistakeable traces of the ordeal; his face was drawn and white'. As the concluding act in this drama unfolded over the succeeding hours, he sat at times 'with bowed head', the confident, sometimes even perky, demeanour of the previous three days of the trial now completely, palpably, drained out of him.

Before he could begin his final speech for the Defence, Mr Johnston had some pieces of incidental business to conclude. These included entering into evidence the death certificate of Bailey's father as a further and firm reminder to the jury of his cause of death – 'acute melancholia and exhaustion'. He also recalled Bailey's sister, Mrs Jennings, to the witness box to engage in this rather enigmatic exchange.

Mr Johnston asked, 'Do you remember your brother coming to Swindon at the beginning of October?'

'Yes.'

'Did you notice anything about his coat?'

'There were a few stains on the back of his coat.'

'Do you know what became of those stains?'

'I handed him a brush, and he brushed them off.'

'You say he brushed them off?'

'Yes.'

Only the dead woman and the prisoner actually knew what happened at Barn Cottage on the night of 29 September, Mr Johnston told the jury near the outset of his three-and-a-half-hour-long address, effectively a plea for Bailey's life. As his wife was beyond recall, Bailey alone could tell them what transpired, he suggested. It was not a question of for *what* purpose Bailey obtained poison but *who*, the jury would have to decide, crucially, actually gave it to Kate. The story Bailey had given them from the witness box was, said Mr Johnston, a true one: that his wife took the poison herself and committed suicide. What stronger proof of her intention and state of mind did they need than Kate's agonised letter to her mother-in-law? It was a letter proved to be in her own handwriting, which Counsel pointedly read out again, slowly and deliberately, to a hushed court.

Mr Johnston then walked the jury minutely through Bailey's life, detailing as much as possible of the good, such as his system of musical notation, for which he had such hopes, yet not shirking mention of the darker recesses of the prisoner's past, including regular breakdowns of his physical and mental health, the latter occasioning a long stay in Banstead Asylum. Mr Johnston made it quite clear to the jury, however, that a defence of insanity was not going to be advanced on the grounds that 'the prisoner was in no way responsible for his wife's death'.

The jury was asked to consider this man who had a keen intelligence, above average as a boy and for the class – Mr Johnston was keen to emphasise – in which he was born. He'd written plays, poetry and brought out inventions; but, when failure beckoned, he'd also contemplated suicide on more than one occasion. But things seemed to be going well for him when he and his family arrived in Bourne End, and he was already much advanced on his musical aspirations hoping they'd earn him some extra money.

In fact, months earlier, Mr Johnston reminded the jury, Bailey had told his sister that the system was complete and he was planning to engage young women to further its cause. As for the notorious advertisement, Bailey had included the 'over 16' line not because he believed cynically that would somehow preclude him from 'the meshes of the criminal law' but because 'those under 16 would be too young and would not make good teachers, canvassers and saleswomen' of his system.

As for his purchase of poisons, that was explained by Bailey's desire to get rid of ants and wasps at his respective rented properties in Bourne End and Little Marlow and also for his intended, legitimate, work as a farrier. Not, Mr Johnston averred, for the purpose of killing his wife so he could have free rein with young women 'for immoral purposes'. Refreshing the jury's memory of just why the Misses Edwards and Marks were invited to sleep over at Barn Cottage, Mr Johnston declared that the latter simply misconstrued Bailey's intentions and had consequently invented her story.

Drawing to a close, Mr Johnston referred back to the letter from Bailey to the Coroner in which he'd written, 'I gave her hers first; then I follow.' This seemed a clear intention that the prisoner was contemplating suicide; but then fearing that Hollie would be unprovided for, he changed his mind.

There is, in fact, no actual record of either Mr Johnston's or Mr Young's speeches in the official Home Office files of the case, so their specific content and exact tenor may only be gleaned from contemporary news reports. One can then merely imagine the gravity with which Mr Johnston surely must have imbued his final entreaty to the jury: that, all through, it had been Bailey's sole aim and ambition to remove the stain of suicide from Kate's name.

It was getting on for 2.30pm when the Court was adjourned for a brief lunch interval after which Mr Young would try to begin to undermine the Defence case, while providing enough evidence 'beyond a reasonable doubt' to secure a 'Guilty' verdict with its terrible consequences. The experienced Counsel's deceptively mild opening – reiterating the necessity, albeit perhaps the inconvenience for both jury and prisoner, of Sunday's hiatus, which had at least obviated the prospect of his starting his closing speech at 10.30pm on a Saturday evening – soon gave way to almost 70 minutes of quietly devastating argument carefully, bit by bit, ripping apart the case for the Defence.

'Lying, lying, lying …' was how Mr Young graphically summed up Bailey's account and evidence – a pack of lies from first to last. From 20 September, when Bailey, fearing he'd lose his work with Mr Hall, absented himself with the fictitious story of a visit to the doctor, the lies really began in earnest, suggested Mr Young. From almost the outset, Prosecuting Counsel was eager to impress upon the jury that there had never been any suggestion that Bailey wasn't responsible for his actions. Insanity had not been put forward as a defence, despite evidence offered about Bailey's father's demise and the prisoner's own irregular mental problems.

It was clear that he knew about the nature of drugs, especially those that were in the house on the afternoon of 29 September. Did Kate commit suicide using the two drugs stramonia and prussic acid? Mr Young suggested firmly to the jury that she did not; that it was actually from her husband's hand she received the fatal doses. The Judge, he said, would direct them as to the point of law regarding the question of a possible suicide pact and one party surviving. Yet, Mr Young was anxious to remind them, until they came into Court had they ever heard one word about Kate committing suicide?

Why the prisoner should have been advised to put forward that plea, after the difficulties he had to face, Mr Young said he couldn't fathom. Why would Bailey sacrifice himself to a charge of murder to shield his dead wife if she committed suicide if he did not want anyone to know that she had committed suicide? So, repeated Mr Young, who gave Kate the drugs, and how were they administered?

After it was alleged that she had taken stramonia, the prisoner, said Mr Young, was very careful to wash up the tea things, in all probability destroying any drug he might have given her, either in her cup of tea or otherwise. Then when she had taken the stramonia, Bailey had told them that he wrote some letters. If what he said were true, added Mr Young, did that not demonstrate callousness on his part? Despite his wife's condition, he not only sat down to write letters but also then left the house to post them.

As for the matter of Kate going to bed – who, asked Mr Young, actually suggested she do so? Once there, it was alleged she then died of prussic-acid poisoning. Who gave her that? There was only Bailey's word for how that was administered. He had given evidence as to what he'd discovered yet never summoned any assistance, either from a neighbour, a doctor or the police. The jury had heard how Bailey had rushed downstairs, found some cotton wool which he doused with chloroform and then, 'cruel as he was', placed it on Kate's nose to help ease her pain. Yet, Mr Young intoned gravely, he made no real attempt to save her.

Mr Young didn't dispute the fact that Bailey truly believed in his system of musical notation, something that was to drive perhaps a terminal wedge in the marriage. In fact, said Mr Young, he was 'crazy' about it – but that didn't make him insane. This growing rift seems to have been manifest in Kate's letter to her mother-in-law. It was, he suggested, the outpourings of a broken heart. Meanwhile, Bailey had his own evil designs in relation to the young women he planned to hire for the alleged purpose of copying and demonstrating his system. When it became clear that the Bourne End house wouldn't suit his real intention, he took Barn Cottage, advertised, gathered his poisons and then kept shuffling appointments and meetings with a clear intention of having an empty house while murder was uppermost in his mind.

A court reporter captured the climactic thrust of Mr Young's speech in this vivid fashion: 'The prisoner had been reckless in his own life and reckless in regard to others. He was a dangerous man, one who had knowledge of drugs – a man who was a danger to the public.' On the evidence given, the jury would have, Mr Young concluded, no hesitation in declaring he was guilty of the charge.

Now past 4.00pm, the light, on what had been already an overcast day outside in Aylesbury with occasional drizzle and a squally wind whipping around the town centre, began also to dim in the court itself, so, as the Judge began his summing up, a couple of candles were placed on the Bench beside him, lending a rather spectral quality to the proceedings.

He began by outlining the law regarding murder and where it pertained to a suicide pact, especially if one of the parties backed out.

'Now, the case for the Defence here is that this woman, Mrs Bailey, took poison of her own free will, on her own initiation, and without any participation by the defendant in the administration of the poison. If that is right, and that is true about her, the defendant is not guilty of murder, because he would have taken no part in the case that led to the woman's death through poison.

'Now the case for the Prosecution is that he gave her poisons without her knowledge, or that he deliberately handed her poisons with her knowledge so that she might die. If you think that he did either of these two things, then the Crown rightly ask you to find him guilty of murder.'

If the contents of the letter to the Coroner were true – that Bailey handed the poison to Kate – then he was guilty of murder. The Defence's version was that, at the time he wrote that letter, Bailey claimed he was attempting to free the 'memory of the dead woman from the aspersion [of suicide] that would rest upon her'.

What then of the 'little green notebook', Exhibit 79, upon which the main pillar of the Defence case, that Kate embarked on voluntary suicide, relied?

'You must deal with it with care, because if it is the writing of his wife, if it is the real writing, and represents the real state of things, it will be of great importance. She says there, "I can't stand it any longer." Later on she says, "It will be the last time where I am concerned, for I shall take jolly good care it is the last time."

'Both Counsel, I think, have assumed that this letter points definitely to suicide, but you must not be so sure about it, as to whether it really points to an intention to commit suicide, and whether it points rather to an intention to leave the prisoner and to have done with him for ever. The word "suicide" is not shown in it. The word "poison" is not shown in it. You have got to consider whether this letter really points to suicide.

'Now, assuming that the wording of the letter points to suicide, still you have got to ask: was this letter an intention, a real intention to commit suicide? This letter you have heard was laid upon a chest of drawers and it was found in August 1920. You must ask yourselves how this came into existence, because you will remember that if his story is right, that this woman committed suicide on 29 September, she left no written message then and this message was written, if at all, in August 1920, a month before.

'Now, you must ask yourselves, does this represent any evident threat of suicide, does it represent any real threat of suicide, or was it merely written to frighten the man, and bring him to a better frame of mind?

'These are rather important questions. Indeed, it may be asked as to whether this, at some time or another, might not have been written as a reality or as a dramatic piece by the woman at the request of the prisoner, in order that something might remain in existence which he could point to as an indication of intention by the woman to commit suicide.'

As if this wasn't already a fairly damning, indeed damaging, piece of theorising on the part of the Judge, then he would surely compound it with the following:

'Ask yourselves further, assuming she wrote this letter at the time as a threat of suicide, were there grounds here, having regard to her health and the terms on which she appeared to be living with this man [nearly seven months pregnant and outwardly happy], that she would, of herself, take away her life by this somewhat hideous method of swallowing prussic acid?

'Now you have heard this evidence, and let me at this point invite you to form your view with regard to the man himself, and say whether you accept his story. You see in the witness box sometimes men of nimble diversity of mind. Is the prisoner a man of this type? You have heard his answers, and explanations and reconciliations of apparently conflicting statements.

'The case for the Crown is that this story by him of voluntary suicide is the invention of an ingenious mind, a plausible mind, and a plausible manner, and is brought forward at this moment, and established in order to save him from the charge of getting rid of the woman who was distasteful to him.'

The Judge then spent the next few minutes reacquainting the jury with almost every aspect of the case that suggested 'voluntary suicide' was the last possible explanation that could be adduced from the available – by which he seemed to imply genuinely reliable – evidence. And systematically, the Judge continued effectively to rubbish every piece of Bailey's version of events:

'His story is the woman lies upon the bed there … with the red liquid of death oozing from her lips. He claims medical knowledge of some sort, and some knowledge of poisons, as he has had experience of attempts at suicide, and knew what steps it was best to take to rid the woman's body of poison, and inducing her to vomit; and yet, he goes downstairs and fetches … chloroform, which in itself is much like poison, puts chloroform to the nose of this woman, not as a remedy, but apparently to mitigate the pangs of this poison, which is seizing her life, and carrying her every moment to her death.

'And then, suppose he had gone back into that room and seen that tragedy, and seen his wife fall back there through this suicide, imagine the horror of the husband, who desired to keep this woman of his alive. The child was there, apparently lying beside the body of the woman, who is slowly growing cold with death. Supposing it had been a case of suicide, voluntary suicide, would you not have thought the man would take the child from the bed, and put it into some other room away from the corpse?'

In the wake of all this, the Judge's next 'what if' scenario, positing instead 'deliberate murder', seemed almost superfluous.

After dealing minutely with Bailey's attempts to obtain poisons and some of the alleged lies he told in pursuit of them, the Judge next moved on to questions of the musical notation, the advertisements, the girls, and the accused's possible motives regarding each, and perhaps all, of them. These he would now lay out for the jury in strangely lurid, even occasionally lascivious, language unlike anything earlier in his otherwise cool, fairly impersonal, summing up:

'The case for the Crown is that this man was subject to these sexual desires. And that he waited until the moment that he had poison and that he was about to embark on the indulgence of these sexual desires.

'If you watch the history of murders, and have been in a court where murder cases have been tried, the men of the jury, at least, will probably have observed how closely the sexual suggestion is interwoven with murder, either by knife, pistol or poison.

'The case for the Crown is that this man poisons his wife in order to take advantage of the position that would follow her death. That he might be free, when she is dead – I am bound to say it – to enjoy the bodies of the women who were coming.'

As has been pointed out before, there is no available transcript of Mr Young's closing remarks, unlike the Judge's, which are meticulously recorded word for word in the Home Office files, so we can only assume – as court reporters also neglected to mention this in their précis of the Prosecution case – that Mr Justice McCardie uttered the following at Counsel's prompting:

'The case for the Crown is this. They say if you look at the way in which his musical system arrangements are made [referring to the wording of the advertisements] you will see deeply concealed the same sexual instinct. It matters not to my mind, you may take a different view, whether he believed in his system or not. It matters not whether the system of music was a good or bad one, whether he believed in it or not … something was necessary for getting girls into the house, touch their hands, watch their bodies and entice them to sleep there.'

The Judge then focused in on the crucial testimony of just one of those girls, Lilian Marks, who had arrived at Barn Cottage as Kate was dying and then spent what the jury had earlier heard was a long, terrifying night trying to resist Bailey's alleged attempts to have 'connection' with her. If the nine men and three women hadn't already been overwhelmed with her dramatic appearance in the witness box, they would be reminded of her supposed ordeal in almost purple terms by the Judge.

'Miss Marks says he [Bailey] spent the night in efforts, in continued efforts, to procure her body. He says this is quite inaccurate, that he did nothing of the sort; all that he did was push her back in order that she should not go into the next room where the dead body of his wife was lying. Now, either the witness Miss Marks is telling the truth or not, either the prisoner is telling the truth or not.

'The difference between them is vital, and if this man is telling a lie as to what happened between himself and Miss Marks, what becomes of his other testimony? Now, you saw him. Is the story Miss Marks has told the truth or not? Is her evidence correct? It is not one of those little points that may be passed in a moment.

'A man may forget, but there are in the life of every woman great crises, and hours she does not forget. They are seared upon the memory, and never forgotten. Can you imagine that any young woman would pass the night, as Miss Marks has told you, trying to resist the efforts of this man to gain her body and make a mistake as to what took place? Why, the whole life and future of the woman was at stake.

'It is not a mere question of attacks made upon her by pushing her by the shoulders and chest; it is the words that were spoken. If Miss Marks is right, he said, "I have come here for a purpose; will you be the mistress of this cottage; will you be the mother of my children?" Which could only mean one thing. Then Miss Marks asks, "Are you married?" He says, "No, I am not married, the child is my sister's child."

'Then there is the curious phrase, which I should think a girl, or at any rate an unmarried woman, would never forget, and she would ever remember. You may be mistaken as to the actual movements on a night but you can scarcely be mistaken as to the phrase used by the man in the course of that night.'

As to any question of Bailey's insanity, the Judge noted that Defence Counsel had made it clear it was not put forward, yet reminded the jury that Mr Johnston had said it was a matter which they ought to consider:

'In my opinion, you ought to consider it, but when you do consider it you must remember the law with regard to insanity. A man is not insane because he wearies of a woman, he is not insane because he lusteth for another woman, a man is not insane because he believes in a foolish system of music, and a man is not insane because he has many peculiarities.

'Before a man can be found guilty but insane, he must suffer from disease of the mind, and the disease must be of such a character as to prevent him, at the time of the act complained of, from knowing what he was doing, and did not even know he was doing wrong. I do not wonder that the learned Counsel for the defendant did not press the point.

'It is true that this man tells us he tried to commit suicide, he might have had sunstroke, he might have had collapse, he might have had injuries to his legs and head. He may, many years ago, have been in Banstead Asylum, but he has never been in an asylum since. Watch the defendant two months before this case, and what sign of insanity was there?'

With the clock moving towards 5.30pm, the Judge, whose scarlet-and-white attire was the only spot of brightness in an otherwise dimly lit courtroom, finally arrived at his closing remarks, which, as was usual in capital cases, included the grave reminder about the enormity of the jury's responsibility together with, on this unique occasion, timely recognition of the historic composition of the 12 men and women.

'This is the first time I have addressed as Judge a jury which also includes three British women. In former days, when men alone formed the jury, I have pointed out to them that a judge often has grave responsibility and extremely arduous duties to perform. The same duties and responsibilities rest on the jury. If you think that he is guilty, you must not flinch from the verdict.

'You must not allow yourselves to escape from a verdict you may dislike merely because you dislike it. In former days, 12 men upheld the law. In the days that are now before us, that law must be upheld by women as well as men. A jury with women in it has to vindicate the difficult law of guarding the security of human life as when the jury was composed of men alone.

'I am told you are the first jury in this country, mixed jury, to adjudicate upon a case of murder. I have told you to the best of my ability the law. I have pointed out to you the facts. I shall now ask you as a British jury of men and women to arrive at your verdict with certainty, and to deliver your verdict with unswerving firmness.'

The media's continuing fascination with the pioneering composition of the jury was expressed best by the *Daily Mail* whose entire coverage of the trial, especially the last day, was viewed, perhaps unsurprisingly, through the prism of its female representation:

'All through the long day, the three women jurors sat almost motionless in the box. Two sat side by side in the centre of the front row. The other sat at the end of the seat and had turned sideways to be more comfortable in the corner. Miss Stevenson, one of the women in the centre, wearing a purple hat and a purple costume, was grimly watchful. Her lips were pursed, her face was immobile for hours on end. Now and again she leant forward; once, she rested her chin on her hands, watching with intent and concentrated eyes the prosecuting Counsel.

'Beside her was Miss White, as sombrely dressed, sad-faced, grey-haired. Round her neck were sable furs; her hands were in a sable muff. She wore a grey costume and a coloured toque. Her expression was watchful, distressed and every now and again she seemed on the verge of swooning. All through the day she listened and watched. Her look of slightly unhappy and purposeful attention never wavered and, like the other two women, she seemed in graven image.'

Miss Stevenson – whom, you may recall, had been asked to be excused at the start of the trial – was the most striking of the three women, and indeed, glowed the *Mail*, she was the dominating figure of the whole jury.

'Certainty' and 'firmness', as requested by the Judge, not to mention the capacity for a blistering turn of speed, seem indeed to have been the residing characteristics of this dauntless dozen, for hardly had everyone taken time to draw breath after the momentous events of the fourth and last day than, just half an hour after Mr Justice McCardie had uttered his final words of guidance, the jury were suddenly back in an eerily silent courtroom. The *Daily Express* wrote: 'His [Bailey's] face was of a dead white paleness, but he stood firmly, his hands grasping the front of the dock. He looked keenly at the jury, particularly the women, whose eyes were downcast.'

As the Judge returned to his seat, there was now placed on the Bench to his left the black cap alongside a pair of white gloves. An equal sense of certainty about how the jury had found now swiftly resonated throughout this corner of the Assize even as the fateful words were being exchanged between the Clerk and the Foreman.

'Do you find the prisoner guilty or not guilty of wilful murder?'

'We find the prisoner guilty of wilful murder.'

'And this is the verdict of you all?'

'Yes.'

The Clerk then turned to Bailey who, it's said, was now looking 'deathly pale', the final ounce of that initial confidence drained out of him, and asked, 'George Arthur Bailey, have you anything to say why the sentence of the Court should not be passed upon you?' To which he replied, cryptically and in, reportedly, low tones, 'I am morally guilty.' Or did he? That was how he was reported in the official shorthand trial transcript. The *Bucks Free Press* and the *Daily Express*, however, reported his actual words as: 'I am not morally guilty.' The *Bucks Herald* noted it simply as: 'I am not guilty.'

The black cap placed upon his head, the Judge, now white-gloved, then passed sentence. 'George Arthur Bailey. The jury have found you guilty of wilful murder. I agree with their verdict. It is my duty to pass sentence upon you according to law. The sentence of the Court upon you is that you be taken from hence to the place from whence you came and then to a place of lawful execution, and that you be hanged by the neck until you be dead, and that your body be afterwards buried within the precincts of the prison in which you last have been confined after your conviction. And may the Lord have mercy on your soul.'

The Chaplain standing alongside the Bench responded with 'Amen'.

As if already resigned to his fate, Bailey quickly turned and disappeared below to the cells before even the warders with him in the dock could assist his passage.

Having dealt summarily with the main actor in this unfolding drama who had now exited below stage, as it were, the Judge next turned to the remaining assembled to draw, he said, their attention to a couple of other matters. First, he wished to commend the Prosecution on the way the case had been so carefully prepared and he singled out three members of the Buckinghamshire Police for special recognition – Supt Kirby (who would eventually become Deputy Chief Constable of the county), Inspector West and PC Poole.

Second, he said he wished to respond to a report contained in one of Saturday's illustrated papers in which it was stated that the women jurors had taken a more 'intelligent interest' in the case than the men, further alleging that one of the male jurors had even been spotted asleep.

The jury, for its own part, had sent the Judge a protest against this allegation, signed by the Foreman, because they considered the insinuation detrimental to the 'interests of British justice'. Mr Justice McCardie said he was glad to receive the note, which also prompted a paean of praise from him to both the men and women of this particular jury. 'I am glad to express my hearty appreciation of the admirable manner in which every member of the jury discharged his or her duties,' he said, while endorsing their protest about such a 'shameful slur'. He then exempted them from further service for five years. The 12, as one, replied, 'Thank you, my lord.'

The proceedings now concluded, the newspapers could reflect on its more unusual aspects without prejudice. Inevitably, the matter of women jurors and their performance was the one that seemed to preoccupy most column inches. Typical was the *Daily Sketch* of 18 January, which, beneath the headline 'WOMEN JURORS MAKE GOOD', reported: 'Women at Aylesbury have disposed finally of the theory that the evidence in certain unpalatable cases is not fit for feminine ears.'

The paper's Special Correspondent noted how, throughout the trial, the Court had been 'crowded with women, most of them young'. He was, he wrote, 'astounded to notice in the gallery a schoolgirl, with her hair flowing over her shoulders. During all the shocking allegations of the prosecution, the detailed examination and cross-examination of the girl witnesses who had dealings with Bailey, she remained in court.' The image clearly remained with him as he later spoke to a woman usher after the end of the trial.

'At first I was inclined to think it wrong,' she confided to me, 'that young girls should attend a case like this but, after all, I have come to the conclusion it may be useful experience for them. The fact that so many women replied to Bailey's advertisement showed that parents are not plain enough with their children, and that girls, perhaps in their ignorance, are too eager to take work in suspicious circumstances. The evidence will open the eyes of the girls present.'

This intriguing little eye-opener from an anonymous court official – quite possibly Mrs Noble who had looked after the women jurors throughout the trial – was then scooped later in the same article by an even more fascinating insight into the mind of at least one of the women jurors, Miss Tack. She told the *Sketch*'s Special Correspondent, 'I think our experience has been extremely interesting. It was my first appearance in a criminal court, and I felt a little – not exactly nervous, for I am not a nervously-disposed person – but a bit out of my element at first.

'I soon settled down, though, and had no difficulty in getting hold of the trend of evidence. The evidence has been very sordid – extremely pitiful, but I don't see any reason why it should not be given in the presence of women. It might be an ordeal to a nervous woman, though. We had to do our best to keep up the spirits of one of the women jurors; occasionally she showed signs of being overcome.'

Miss Tack was also interviewed by the *Daily Mail* for her opinion of the trial: 'It did not upset me at all. I have looked after sick people, and I work with five brothers on a farm. I just listened to all I heard and used my judgement as well as I could. It has been a very broadening experience. I see no reason at all why women should not serve on juries, though I think they should be over 50. They have a settled mind then. There should always be more than one woman on a jury, but in a way, I prefer men. They get more to the point somehow.'

The *Daily Express* summed it up by saying: 'The women showed unmoved faces and well-scheduled nerves while all the grim business of the Judge's black cap and the Chaplain's "Amen" to the sentence was in progress. They had strung themselves to that point with deliberate fortitude. They came through the ordeal of verdict and sentence as bravely as any one of the men.'

In its short account of the final day, the *Times* couldn't resist closing with its own dry take on the mixed-jury phenomenon: 'It was still noticeable today that Counsel have not yet become used to addressing a mixed jury. Mr Hugo Young KC, in his speech for the Prosecution, addressed them as "Members of the jury" at first but soon slipped back into the familiar "Gentlemen". Occasionally, he remembered to refer to them as "Gentlemen … and ladies". The Judge, on the other hand, referred to them punctiliously throughout as "Members of the jury".'

The Judge still had one more important piece of trial business to conclude while the public and jury weaved their way homeward and as Bailey was being escorted by railway back to HM Prison Oxford. In the upstairs drawing room of the elegant Judge's Lodgings, Mr Justice McCardie sat down to compose the following letter:

To The Home Secretary

Sir, R v George Arthur Bailey

I beg to inform you that this man was today found guilty of the murder of his wife on Sept 29/30 and was sentenced to death by me.

The case for the prosecution was that he administered prussic acid to her whereby she died.

It is clear she was killed through prussic acid. The case for the defence was that Mrs Bailey committed suicide without the aid or consent of the condemned man (cf exhibit 79 Aug/20)

The case is curious both in its facts and its psychology. The evidence was voluminous. The circumstances were complicated. The body of the dead woman was found by the police on Oct 2/20 and at a house occupied by the o/f and known as Barn

Cottage. The o/f was arrested at Reading on the same day. He was charged with the murder of his wife. Neither then or until the trial did he say she had committed suicide.

Upon him (when arrested) were found 4 bottles of poison including a bottle of prussic acid of which a part of the contents had been used.

There was also found upon him a document (exhibit 48) in his own writing in which he stated that he 'had handed the poison to his wife and that she had believed his statements'. He also said (in a later passage) 'I gave her stramonia first and then hydrocyanic acidic prussic acid.'

The case for the Crown was that the statements in this document were correct and were corroborated by many other circumstances and documents. The o/f said in his evidence that the document was not correct and that his reason for signing the document was he had given the poison because he wanted to free the memory of his wife from the blot of voluntary and unaided suicide.

I think myself that the o/f wrote the document at a time when he intended to kill himself with the poisons in his possession. It was written about two days after the crime and just before his arrest. It was addressed to the Coroner.

For by now the o/f had become weary of his wife and wanted to get rid of her. He had described her as 'common'. He had without valid excuse got diverse poisons from a chemist by means of false statements. He had formed, I think, a strong sexual desire for other women. It would take too long to detail the facts of this unusual case.

I am satisfied that the o/f did administer the poison to the dead woman and that he told her that he himself would commit suicide so that he might follow her to death.

The o/f is a clever, ingenious and plausible man. He has

a bad criminal record. The defence of insanity was not actually raised. I think that he was perfectly sane at the time of the murder.

But he has a curious mental history – had several times tried to commit suicide, had suffered from sunstroke, had been in an asylum and had suffered from falls which injured his legs and his head.

The case is one of the most unusual which has been tried before me. I agree with the verdict of the jury.

I am

Yours faithfully

Later that week, the *Bucks Advertiser and Aylesbury News*, one of the longer established of the local papers that still flourished in those days, delivered its own verdict on the trial, calling it 'one of the most remarkable heard in the old Courthouse of the County Hall', and on Bailey, in particular: 'No one present at the trial could quarrel with the verdict of "Guilty". The prisoner, Bailey, in the witness box displayed a cool and calculating mind, which, considering the issue at stake, was most uncanny and repugnant. Listening to his evidence was like having cold water poured down one's spine. It is hardly necessary to remind my readers that this was the first occasion on which a mixed jury of men and women has been empanelled to try a charge of murder. They must have been rather tired of being reminded of the fact in other ways.'

10

'DON'T LET
MY MUSIC DIE'

A month to the day after leaving the dock for the final time at Bucks Assizes, Bailey was back in Court, but this time the judicial setting was the altogether more austere Royal Courts of Justice, commonly known as the Law Courts, on the Strand in London. It was St Valentine's Day – although there was a distinct lack of love in the air – when Bailey stepped into the dock of the Lord Chief Justice's Court shortly after 10.30am on 14 February. Ranged before him were the three Judges who would hear his Appeal that day: Mr Justice Greer, Mr Justice Sankey and, presiding, Mr Justice Avory, whose nickname 'The Hanging Judge' must have done precious little to improve the spirits of Bailey and his returning Counsel, Mr Johnston.

Sir Horace Edmund Avory was now 70, and had once been described as 'thin-lipped, cold, utterly unemotional, silent and humourless, and relentless towards lying witnesses and brutal criminals', and, separately, 'he holds the scales of justice in skinny, attenuated hands'.

Observing the prisoner for the first time since the four-day trial at Aylesbury, the correspondent for the *Bucks Free Press* was clearly taken aback by Bailey's appearance this time round. 'He had aged considerably, and there were visible traces on his countenance of the strain which he had undergone. His smile, which had been a feature all through the trial, had vanished.'

In concert with his solicitors, Bailey had formulated four grounds of Appeal – 'that there was misdirection by the Judge to the jury in that he did not place before the jury the possibility of the truth of my Defence, but so emphasised the case for the Crown as almost to obscure my Defence, and at the end of the Summing Up used emphatic expressions which could only be construed as a direction that I was guilty … that the Judge failed clearly to direct the jury on the possibility and probability of my wife having committed suicide … that the verdict was against the weight of evidence … and that I am not guilty of the offence charged.'

Presenting the case for Bailey, Mr Johnston said that Kate's death by prussic-acid poisoning was not disputed but the defence was that the prisoner did not administer it to her. The Prosecution, he said, relied on Bailey's letter to the Coroner which Bailey said subsequently was not true and was written because he wished to clear the reputation of his dead wife of the slur that would be cast upon her by having committed suicide. Mr Johnston then pointed out a past history of suicidal tendencies in Bailey's family.

Mr Justice Avory then made the first of many interventions – Mr O'Sullivan, deputising for Hugo Young on behalf of the Crown, was barely required to contribute throughout – asking Mr Johnston in relation to Bailey's note to the Coroner, 'There is also this passage: "Please that God will forgive her. Forgive me …" What did God have to forgive her for?'

'Suicide, I suppose.'

'Did he not say at one time, "Although I am an Atheist, it came across my mind that we should be parted for ever"?'

'I admit that the prisoner did say that while detained at Marlow Police Court.'

Mr Johnston pressed on with his case, explaining that Bailey had purchased the poisons for his farrier work. As for the employment of young women, this was not part of some concerted scheme for their seduction and to enable him to murder his wife, but merely to assist Bailey in his system of musical notation; he also wished to make it clear to their Lordships that the poisons had been bought 'some considerable time' before Bailey engaged them for his notation – a point, claimed Mr Johnston, not accurately put by Mr Justice McCardie to the jury at Aylesbury. It was, in fact, also over three weeks before Kate's death that Bailey had written to Miss Parsons, the photographer's assistant, who had lived at the same house in Bourne End, for some cyanide of potassium to tackle the wasps' nests in the wall of Millbrook.

That, incidentally, should have been emphasised in the singular – wasp's nest – Mr Johnston explained.

'How can you say it should have been in the singular when Bailey in his letter said there were several wasps' nests?' queried Mr Justice Avory.

This then led to an arcane albeit rather pivotal exchange between them concerning ants and/or wasps at Millbrook, and wasps at Barn Cottage. Mr Johnston said Bailey knew of the existence of wasps' nests at Barn Cottage before he left Millbrook and had clearly muddled up the location of the respective insects in his missive to Miss Parsons. Miss Boney, daughter of Barn Cottage's landlady, had told the trial that she wasn't aware of any wasps' nests there, while admitting she hadn't been in the garden; the evidence of next-door-neighbour Mrs Hester and others was that there were such things at the property. This point, a hugely significant one and a reasonable explanation, Mr Johnston declared, should have been pointed out to the jury.

It seems, though, that Mr Johnston need hardly have bothered with the foregoing, for Mr Justice Avory appeared blinkered to such an explanation, reflecting dismissively, 'If the letter to Miss Parsons is true, then the excuse for obtaining the cyanide of potassium is not true because there were no wasps' nests at Millbrook at the time the appellant wrote the letter.'

Undeterred, Mr Johnston reiterated why Bailey required poisons – in order, generally, to carry out farriery work of which he had considerable knowledge. He had been brought up among cattle and had worked on farms. More recently, having served a milk round with some 300 customers and knowing some of them apparently wished to have cats and dogs put down, he thought he could supplement his income by destroying them. That was a reasonable explanation for their possession, said Mr Johnston, and, if there was any doubt in the minds of the jury as to the truth of Bailey's statement, he should have been given benefit of it.

The Defence also wanted to refute the Crown's contention that Bailey's sole purpose with his 'bogus system' of notation was to lure young women for the purpose of seducing them and that he did indeed 'carry out his designs on one of the engaged girls'. Inadmissible, urged Mr Johnston, as was allegation against the prisoner of a serious assault, an entirely different offence from the official charge of murder, which also should not have been allowed to go to the jury. He then quoted a previous judgment, which he thought backed his case. Mr Justice Avory was once again dismissive.

After the pair had continued to debate the matter of timings concerning the various comings and goings of the girls as well as plans for their possible sleepovers, Mr Johnston then broached the question of evidence given by two doctors for the Crown: that it would be impossible for a person to take the two poisons – stramonia and hydrocyanic – without knowing what they were. It was clear that Kate knew her husband had purchased the poisons, because she was with him when he visited Mr King's shop in Marlow and made the purchases.

'She knew that he was purchasing them for veterinary purposes?' asked Mr Justice Avory.

'Yes,' replied Mr Johnston, 'and our point is that, if the poison was taken at all, she took it voluntarily; that it could not have been given to her in her sleep; and that it could not have been administered to her in either food or drink without detection.'

'Do you say she agreed to commit suicide?'

'Yes. Some time before.'

'When did she agree to do that?'

'About three years ago – before her baby was born.'

'The letter,' Mr Justice Avory continued, 'addressed to the Coroner, is a very important one. Do you not say that they both agreed to commit suicide?'

'There is something, certainly, to justify that view, but I suggest that Mrs Bailey committed suicide and the prisoner was "to follow".'

"'I handed the poison to her ...'" Mr Justice Avory snapped back. 'How is that going to be construed into evidence that the prisoner was to follow her, if she took the poison of her own free will? It seems to me there was some justification for the learned Judge at the Assizes to have asked that question.'

Mr Johnston then argued that the point was used by Mr Justice McCardie to prejudice the case, and that he should have warned the jury that the prisoner had made a certain statement and that they should not have paid any attention to it.

Mr Justice Avory then asked, 'How was the prisoner going to clear himself of murder in order to clear his wife of the stigma of suicide?'

That was the point, continued Mr Johnston. 'I say the Judge should not have paid any attention whatever to that.' The Judge, continued Mr Johnston, was equally culpable in respect of the evidence given by Lilian Marks and should have given Bailey the fullest assistance. She had admitted in cross-examination that she didn't tell the police her story until about a fortnight after the alleged occurrence and it was more than probable, Counsel alleged, that she hadn't given the true version as to the prisoner's intentions and meaning. Miss Marks had, after all, plenty of time to leave Barn Cottage on the morning of 30 September, yet she didn't do so until 10.45am.

'And went straight away and complained,' countered Mr Justice Avory.

'Very likely, but it does not show that there was anything in the nature of a serious assault committed on her because she went to a clergyman and not to the police. The prisoner's story was that he stayed in Miss Marks' room during the night in order to keep her from going into the room in which his dead wife was lying.'

Mr Justice Avory suggested, 'The simplest way out of the difficulty would have been for the prisoner to have told Miss Marks that she could not stay in the house and that she had better go home.'

'Perhaps so … There is no doubt that at that time the prisoner was in a state of great distress of mind.'

'And Bailey opened the door to her, showed her upstairs to her room, which was next to the one in which the dead woman was lying.'

'I say that as Miss Marks' evidence was not put into writing immediately after the occurrence, it was impossible for her to give exactly what took place, and what in her view was the prisoner's motive. It was easy for his words to be misconstrued.'

Mr Justice Avory continued, '"How would you like to be mistress of a house like this?" is one question he is alleged to have asked her.'

'That does not show he means this house – Barn Cottage.'

Asked by Mr Justice Avory about the bruises on her legs, arm and chest, Mr Johnston said that they were admitted but only sustained, according to Bailey, when he was trying to prevent Miss Marks from checking out Kate's death chamber, not from trying to prevent the prisoner from clambering into her bed during the night. There was no evidence, insisted Mr Johnston, that Bailey actually took advantage of Miss Marks.

For the brief remainder of his case on behalf of Bailey, Mr Johnston tried as he could to make out that some of the points had not been put by the Judge as fairly on the prisoner's behalf as they were for the Crown, before concluding, perhaps a little weakly, 'I think that the prisoner's story was as probable as the other.' He then added cryptically, 'There is a probability of the case going before another authority but I would rather not go into that, or give any other particulars just now.' This seemed to be a veiled suggestion that an appeal to the Home Secretary on the grounds of insanity was to be lodged imminently.

A colleague once wrote of Sir Horace Avory, 'one tries in vain to read the workings of the mind behind that mask-like face'. If his mind remained unreadable during the first part of the Appeal, his words at least were about to be uttered for all to hear as he delivered the judgment of the Court. Surrounded by three warders, Bailey stood up in the dock to await this latest moment of truth. Toying with the dock rail, he only occasionally lifted his head in the direction of the three Judges.

Mr Justice Avory, said to have sentenced to death more people than any other Judge of his day, began with a résumé of the main evidence relating to the discovery of Kate's body and Bailey's efforts to obtain various poisons. He then dealt carefully with the aftermath of her death and the increasing web of lies spun by the prisoner when dealing with everybody from the clergyman Reverend Allen (to whom Lily Marks had complained) to his own sister, Mrs Jennings, in Swindon.

He read out the notorious Coroner's letter followed by Bailey's subsequent statement at Marlow Magistrates' Court, 'where he set up a totally different story'. The story changed yet again, said Mr Justice Avory, when Bailey gave evidence at Bucks Assizes. 'One would have thought that if his wife had committed suicide he would have gone at once to the police; that he did not do, but left the neighbourhood.'

On the evidence before them, they – that is, he and his

fellow Judges – could not see how it was possible for the jury to come to any other conclusion than the prisoner had murdered his wife by poisoning her, even taking into account the story of a possible suicide pact that might have gone wrong. The law on that matter had been correctly spelled out by Mr Justice McCardie.

> 'The only reasonable inference was that, on 29 September, Mrs Bailey had drunk tea which her husband had prepared. The prisoner had introduced poison [stramonia] into the tea; had then persuaded her to go to bed; and had taken advantage of her condition to administer prussic acid because the prisoner had told them [the jury] himself that after drinking the tea his wife had complained of a burning sensation at the back of the throat. Whether he had also chloroformed her, one could not say, for the purpose of getting her out of the way so as to leave him clear to have the girls in the house.'

If they hadn't suspected it before, Bailey and his Counsel must by now have guessed that the wind was blowing just one way.

Mr Justice Avory, moving in for the final kill, as it were, now ruled on the admissibility or otherwise of certain evidence, most specifically in the matter of Miss Marks and her tale of attempted seduction. Precedent deemed that in every charge of murder it was always an issue before the jury whether the accused had a motive for the commission of the crime and evidence of that was always admissible.

> 'The prisoner visited her room during the night, and her evidence was consistent with the case put forward by the

Crown that the prisoner did attempt to seduce her. The next morning Miss Marks got up, went downstairs, and certainly they had breakfast together, but as soon as she could conveniently do so, and not wishing to arouse suspicion, she left the house quietly and went to Reverend Allen and there made a complaint of him [Bailey]. The evidence of Miss Marks was perfectly admissible and clearly showed the existence of a motive.'

As to any question of insanity, the evidence, said Mr Justice Avory, suggested the appellant knew perfectly well the nature and quality of the act he was doing when he poisoned his wife. The Appeal would be dismissed. According to the *Bucks Free Press*, Bailey 'staggered when he heard the result, and almost stumbled out of the dock assisted by the warders'.

Within a day, maybe even hours, Bailey, by now back at Oxford Prison, seems to have regained enough composure for one final bid to escape the noose. On an official Petition form for the attention of 'The Right Honourable His Majesty's Principal Secretary of State for the Home Department', dated 16 February, he hand-wrote an extraordinary, rambling screed in two sections separated by some poetry, in which he attempted to refute the judgment of their Lordships, explain his *modus operandi* and, possibly, try also to persuade the Home Secretary that he was indeed legally mad.

This, in full, is his Petition, never before published, which perhaps provides the most accurate and telling insight of all into the mind of someone Mr Justice McCardie had described as a 'clever, ingenious and plausible man'. Unless, of course, it was purely intended as Bailey's ultimate bluff. Apart from breaking it down in shorter, more readable paragraphs, the (lack of) punctuation is as originally penned:

Sir,

When I petitioned you to grant me Legal Aid, charged with murder and attempted rape, I told you that my own conduct had built up a well of evidence around me, which must be pulled down, else I was practically committing suicide; I suppose what I ought to have written should have been 'or the Government will be practically committing murder'.

I know I have been a liar, before Arrest but have the Prosecution proved me to be one during the Proceedings in connection with my defence: how sick and tired I am of all this twaddle dealing with the sexual instinct, the desire to gain possessive control over young girls, what if I did advertise like I did, it was for everyone to see, to weed out undesirables, to prevent an avalanche of replies from unsuitable applicants, how do they account for the lapse of time from the first Advt to the second.

I am weary of continually telling my story which is branded as lies simply because of my past, a past in which I have had to tell lies to gain an honest livelihood, and yet out of these so called lies how eagerly they fix on what they want to believe for their own purpose twisting its meaning around and ignoring the rest of these so called lies.

What if my wife did complain that the tea made her throat burn, ask the Doctors to repeat their evidence, did I not have tea at the same time, was it not the drinking of tea after drinking stramonium that caused her throat to hurt, how can I tell you every word, every detail of what happened when even now memory keeps coming back, which I wish to God did not.

I am content to ignore the evidence of Miss Marks. My wife and I were one, she could see me on the wrong path, you know her life history with me, the tragedy of Winchester, would any woman see it repeated, rather than have me taken from her again, for her to bring another child into the world under conditions similar to the last, where are men's senses, do you wonder that I refused to answer Counsel's question at the Trial, for the [word here unreadable], did they think I was knave, coward, enough to reveal such facts.

I would rather do again a hundred times (rather than let the public know) what I done at the trial, and even at the Appeal Court, what does the average man know of such love as ours, how can I explain my letter to the Coroner, why should I, all I want is justification for our Babs, the horror of these happenings removed from my people, my wife understands, and tells me what to do although she would have me with her and I would rather go, does it not seem peculiar that I a liar and continued would be suicide, and I have made more than three attempts, have resisted the awful temptation since arrest, and have faced my trial and my appeal and now face you, is that the conduct of a man who resorts to suicide whenever in difficulties.

My beloved, and God knows and understands I could not face it and live if my Kit was not helping me. Can they not see that what I hated to do at first, I have nerved myself to do now why should I not take all the blame, did I not tell Justice McCardie that I was morally guilty, can I say more. You know my history yet, would I prostitute this music worked out patiently, with promise of a great future, honourable name to such a vile, dishonourable revolting object. I sometimes think the world must be mad and not me to believe such a nightmare.

Let her rest; the weary night. Never brought her dreams like this

Let her sleep; the morning light Shall not wake her from her bliss.

Glad was she to end the fight; Death has conquered with a kiss.

Tired eyes need watch no more; Flagging feet, the race is run;
Hands that heavy burdens bore; Set them down, the day
is done;
Heart be still — through anguish sore; Everlasting peace is
won.

Ah see — here are the fragments of my shattered pile!
I keep them, and the flowers that sprang between
Their broken workmanship — the flowers and the weeds;
Sleep soft among the violets, Oh my Queen —
Lie calm among my ruined thoughts and deeds.

What is death — to him who meets it with an upright heart?
A quiet haven where the shattered bark,
Harbours secure till the rough storm be past
Yet see you smile, that wistful smile, those eyes,
How for our babe thy spirit bids me strive;
Our Babs, harbinger of all that life held dear,
Leading me on with courage, killing fear.
Life appearing void, fanned by new desire,
Your second self, of thee, to guard from Devils mire
G.A. Bailey
As soon as the fatality occurred I knew my word was
worthless, I suppose it is so now.

I am, Sir,
Your Humble Servant
George A. Bailey

Continuation of Petition 15.02.21

Sir
I do not wish you to believe any of my defence for my sake
as far as I am concerned physically, this life this world matters

nothing to me; my Counsel is in possession of my full life history. I have had enough. I don't suppose since Xmas 1907 that I have had a moment's perfect peace and freedom of mind and since December 1909, have been continually in pain and anxiety, but it does not matter to our child as to whether the course of events will continue in their present direction.

My beloved desires me to cast off this worn out material body to go with her and yet how sadly persuades me to fight on for Babs but ever to stay with me and help me in the bitterness of my life. Was Inspector West, Superintendent Kirby men, men in the true sense of the word to allow me to go on like I did knowing everything.

Is my evidence, my statement at the Police Court Proceedings at Marlow a mass of contradictions as put by Mr Justice Avory. I smile and yet how bitterly when I think of my three hundred customers, me asking all their daughters to take up this music, asking the factory girls from the numerous factories at Bourne End to take it up, the sexual instinct, the sexual desire, I could have glutted myself without advertising, without the so called aid of an alleged worthless system (proved to be the opposite).

I kept nothing back from my beloved, my past she knew; my hopes and fears she shared — her influence she endeavoured to wield and with partial success, but oh heavens it was like having a gold mine in the back garden and not being able to dig it out. Witnesses, yes, not two or three but 60; not one letter but scores could have been produced. They said I called my wife common. I have my explanation, need I have done so, could I not have left my letter unexplained, common, mad fools, uncommon. Trying to get me to sell my music to 'John Bull' trying to persuade in every way to give up my extravagant ideas and conduct, I can see it now.

Even if I had done what the Prosecution say I ought to have done, would that have helped me, I did not desire to, why should I when my, our world had ceased to exist, would I have been believed, or would I have been laughed at and still be in this position. How is it I was not questioned on the 'horrible things' I mentioned in letter; shall I tell you what they were, do you want telling. Did I not mention Babs, did I not purchase 2 gallons of oil that week.

Yes I can remember some things, and how tempted, I resisted temptation, how when the fatality occurred, I fought for time, gain time to think, think, think what to do and can you wonder at my expression horrible things, and yet my beloved would not let me return to Marlow after all to carry out my intentions. Lies, yes, all lies. I suppose these are lies, and yet have I ever told lies at my previous convictions when doing well and things going, for me fairly smoothly puts me in mind of the old fable of the little boy who continually cried wolf.

However, let it be, my responsibility ceases with the forwarding of this petition: desiring death I fight it, not in my own strength but my Kit's, and God understands it all. Cold blooded, callous hearted, yes when I put on the rhinoceros hide, the elephant skin, to face the world and its kicks. I think sometimes that soft-heartedness, susceptibility to the finer feelings has hurt more than the kicks.

Did I not state that my wife's hand was shaking when she poured out the tea, did I not volunteer all these statements. Could they shake me in my cross examination insinuating lies, putting false and other ideas into my lips, suggesting my wife was not young enough for me, I was going to cut her into pieces, yet after all, I can but treat it with contempt, how about the evidence of Mr Day, wilful, malicious perjury – why was he not produced at the Assizes, look up the Police Court and Inquest

depositions, what relation is he to Miss Marks, ask the public at
Wycombe and Aylesbury.
  I am, Sir, your humble servant
  George A. Bailey

[When originally reproduced in the local paper, Bailey's verse also made reference to two other poets, M Macleod and Lord Lytton. What might have been their original lines, or what was perhaps intended as his homage to them, is not at all clear.]

Bailey's missive to the Home Secretary was quickly followed by one, briefer and more to the point, from his brother Thomas, which 'solemnly and sincerely' petitioned the Minister 'to consider the prerogation of mercy on the grounds that he [George] is and has been for a number for years totally and absolutely insane and completely mentally and morally incapable of appreciating and recognizing the enormity of crime and of authority, human or divine.'

What the no-nonsense Tynesider the Rt Hon Edward Shortt PC KC, once a practising barrister and part-time Judge before he became Home Secretary in David Lloyd George's Liberal Cabinet, must have made of all this is not officially recorded. All that was reported in response was a brief 'The Home Secretary refused to intervene'.

Bailey had already spent four-and-a-half months in Oxford Prison by the time he returned from London to face just under three weeks more there before he was due to be executed. By all accounts, he was a model prisoner, albeit protesting his innocence throughout. As well as frequently corresponding with his solicitors, he also had several visits from the prison's Wesleyan chaplain, Mr Gearey.

On the afternoon before his appointed execution, Mr Wood visited Bailey and received instructions about the upbringing of Hollie and what the *Bucks Free Press* reported as 'certain confidential communications with regard to the crime and other matters'. In words, however, that can only have come directly from Mr Wood himself, the prisoner was said to be 'very calm and quite resigned to his fate'. Bailey's final words to Mr Wood were: 'Don't let my music die.'

11

LIFE FOR A LIFE

Shortly before 8.00am on a cloudy, damp Wednesday morning, a little over six weeks after sentence had been passed on Bailey at Aylesbury, the small crowd that had assembled outside Oxford Prison were galvanised by the sight of a white handkerchief waving from the window of the condemned cell, an indication, the newspapers reported, that 'Bailey was in good spirits in face of the doom he was shortly to meet.' The handkerchief was waved twice and then disappeared. At 8.07am, three warders came out and posted this sign on the prison doors:

Declaration of Sheriff and others
We the undersigned, hereby declare that Judgement of Death was this day executed on George Arthur Bailey in his Majesty's Prison of Oxford in our presence.

Dated this 2nd day of March
FH Parrott, Under-Sheriff of Buckinghamshire
Wm Brown, Governor of said Prison
Edward Gearey, Wesleyan Chaplain of said Prison
Cert of Surgeon, RH Sankey MB
Signed off by Henry Galpin, Coroner of Oxford

The final judicial rites in Bailey's life had effectively begun some 16 hours earlier with the arrival on the Tuesday at the prison of the senior hangman John Ellis at around 4.00pm, as was his usual custom, accompanied, on this occasion, by one of his regular assistants, Edward Taylor. Before retiring for an early night in the quarters assigned to him and Taylor, Ellis had the task of sorting out the actual logistics of the hanging itself, which mainly involved the length of rope that would be required as well as calculating a suitable drop for a man of Bailey's stature.

The heavier the condemned man, the shorter Ellis made the drop; conversely, the lighter the man (or woman), the longer the drop, to an absolute maximum of 10ft, remembering that the total length of a drop under a trapdoor was usually 12ft. These decisions were absolutely crucial ones because if, as Ellis wrote helpfully in his memoirs, 'the hangman underestimates the drop, the victim will not die at once of a broken neck, which is the object of modern hanging methods, but will be strangled. If, on the other hand, he overestimates, the resultant jerk can pull the victim's head off.'

After viewing Bailey discreetly through the inspection hole of the condemned cell as well as having to hand his vital statistics – 5ft 4½in, 143lb (his weight in clothing having been taken for this purpose earlier that day) with, what would be officially documented later, 'a short, muscular neck' – Ellis calculated the optimal length of drop at 7ft 1in.

His next task was to inspect the scaffold situated in a chamber, often referred to, rather crassly, as the 'execution suite'. The room, which was usually formed from two 10ft by 6ft single prison cells, contained the large trapdoor generally double-leaved; in Oxford's case, it was single-leaved. The wooden beam from which the rope was suspended was usually set into the walls of the chamber above, with a section of the floor removed. Being of an old 19th-century type, the chamber at Oxford had, however, its beam simply set into the walls of the chamber just above head height. Ellis's habit was to test the scaffold itself by fastening a rope around a sandbag then dropping it; the sandbag would be left dangling until the morning of the execution so as to take the stretch out of the rope.

Ellis would also have carefully noted that HM Prison Oxford also differed from his other more regular haunts – from Leeds to Pentonville, Lancaster Castle to Chelmsford – in another important aspect. With newer chambers, a lobby area of no more than 15ft usually separated the condemned cell from the gallows, significantly reducing the distance the prisoner would have to walk between the two. However, Oxford's dated set-up meant a longer final walk than usual down a corridor before turning left into the 'execution suite'.

The following morning, Ellis got up at around 5.30am, had a hot cup of tea and went to the chamber for final arrangements. Then, at approximately 6.40am, he took another look through the inspection hole to check on Bailey in his cell. Back to the scaffold for some last-minute tinkering before one final peep at the condemned man. Bailey, meanwhile, according to the *Maidenhead Advertiser*, 'rose early and breakfasted well'. He had also carefully written in pencil on his slate the following:

Men, if life means nothing to you, death means nothing to you, why do you continue to live? If life which is so rough for you at times is still so sweet, and Death, which appears to be such a relief thought of, why do you wish to live? And why do you fear to die?

Brothers, I have been counting the hours, the minutes that separate me from Death. I have passed through Hell, such Hell as I hope and pray God will never come to any of you. The Hell of a tortured mind, of a racked conscience, the Hell of physical fear of Death. I have passed through the Hell, a Hell of fire of ruined chances, of regrets, a Hell of remorse. I have laughed, sneered, scoffed, mocked at God, ridiculed the idea of there being a God.

Chums, read the Psalms for today, the day I pay the supreme penalty for crime committed. You know that deep down in your heart of hearts, a voice cries out to you, Fool! Fool! Old chaps, you may bluff yourself for a time, trying to convince yourself by your arguments that you are Right. But ever remember, comrades, that God is God and never bluffed.

If only I could burn it into your minds, hammer it into your hearts, with a thousand ton hammer that Bluff fails when Death asks its question, are you satisfied with your belief? I have had to answer that question, and I have been worse than you, more pigheaded and puffed up in my arguments, harder than the diamond.

I have had to face God with my hands foul, Black! My people brokenhearted, my little Babs an orphan, my aged mother (a mother in a thousand) crushed by my iniquity. Could I have faced Death, Death with all this stabbing into me, could

*you? If there was no God, but only your misery, wretchedness
and the Devil's laughter, left to you? It is the Devil that bluffs
and I know.*

When the Governor, William Brown, visited Bailey for the
first time that morning, the prisoner handed him the slate,
asking if it could be read to the other inmates when they were
all together in chapel. Brown told him he'd read it first and
then 'consider the matter'. Bailey seemed satisfied with that,
saying, 'I will leave the matter entirely in your hands,
Governor, and please use your discretion as regards reading it
or destroying it.'

Befitting its possible future use in chapel for the spiritual
wellbeing of his fellow prisoners, he'd also listed some suitable
hymns and readings to accompany his carefully chosen words,
beginning with Hymn 608:

*Through the night Thy angels kept
Watch beside me while I slept;
Now the dark has passed away,
Thank Thee, Lord, for this new day.
North and south and east and west
May Thy holy name be blest;
Everywhere beneath the sun,
As in Heaven, Thy will be done.
Give me food that I may live;
Every naughtiness forgive;
Keep all evil things away
From Thy little child this day.*

Then, he wrote, there should be Hymn 601:

Lord, I would own Thy tender care,
And all Thy love to me;
The food I eat, the clothes I wear,
Are all bestowed by Thee.
'Tis Thou preservest me from death
And dangers every hour;
I cannot draw another breath
Unless Thou give me power.
Kind angels guard me every night,
As round my bed they stay:
Nor am I absent from Thy sight
In darkness or by day.
My health, and friends, and parents dear,
To me by God are giv'n;
I have not any blessing here
But what is sent from Heav'n.
Such goodness, Lord, and constant care,
I never can repay;
But may it be my daily prayer,
To love Thee and obey.

The first of two readings was to be from the First Book of John, Chapter Two, beginning: 'My little children, these things write I unto you, that ye sin not. And if any man sin, we have an advocate with the Father, Jesus Christ the righteous …' But he didn't specify whether it was to be in part or all of the subsequent 28 verses.

Finally, Bailey requested Psalm 14:

The fool hath said in his heart, There is no God. They are corrupt, they have done abominable works, there is none that doeth good.

The Lord looked down from heaven upon the children of men, to see if there were any that did understand, and seek God.

They are all gone aside, they are all together become filthy: there is none that doeth good, no, not one.

Have all the workers of iniquity no knowledge? who eat up my people as they eat bread, and call not upon the Lord.

There were they in great fear: for God is in the generation of the righteous.

Ye have shamed the Counsel of the poor, because the Lord is his refuge.

Oh that the salvation of Israel were come out of Zion! when the Lord bringeth back the captivity of his people, Jacob shall rejoice, and Israel shall be glad.

In a letter to the Home Office, dated 5 March – three days after the execution – Brown enclosed the wording of Bailey's peroration, suggesting, 'I do not think it advisable that such should be read, as suggested, and forward copy to you for your consideration, and instructions, if any.'

The reply came back to him two days after that: 'Clearly this effusion should not be read to other prisoners.'

At around 7.55am, Ellis and Taylor met up with the rest of the execution party led by the Under-Sheriff, Mr Parrott, and Governor Brown. After brief introductions, Ellis then pushed open Bailey's cell door, made sure his shirt was open at the neck, patted him on the shoulder and probably muttered a few words of encouragement. Then the group, with Ellis heading swiftly to the front, moved together down the corridor towards the chamber. In the old days, the executioner had always walked behind the condemned man but, from 1910, three years after he had become senior hangman, Ellis instituted a new procedure at the execution of Dr Crippen, who had been similar in height and weight to Bailey. Ellis therefore sped on ahead, leaving the prisoner with the rest of the execution party, so he was waiting at the scaffold when they arrived. Ellis wrote later, 'Thus time was saved and avoidance of confusion on the scaffold was noticeable.'

A minute or so after 8.00am, Taylor quickly pinioned Bailey's legs while Ellis slipped a white cap and noose over his head. Taylor sprang clear of the trapdoor and Ellis pulled the lever.

The *Maidenhead Advertiser* reported that 'the culprit displayed very great coolness and courage during the short distance that had to be traversed from the condemned cell to the scaffold ... Ellis, the executioner, was so expeditious in carrying out his arrangements that but very few seconds elapsed before the drop fell. Death was instantaneous.' The *Bucks Advertiser and Aylesbury News* told its readers that Bailey 'had shown no emotion. He left no confession but had responded to the ministrations of the Prison Chaplain.'

As the law then demanded, the body was left hanging for one hour. According to prison records: 'The length of the drop measured after the execution, from the level of the floor of the scaffold to the heels of the suspended culprit [was] 7ft 4in.' That is, 3in longer than Ellis's predetermined estimate. The cause of death was, officially, '(a) dislocation of [upper cervical] vertebrae; (b) asphyxia'.

Just after 9.00am, Ellis and Taylor took the body down and prepared it for autopsy. Having tidied the gallows and packed the rest of the equipment back into the execution boxes, they were then free to leave the prison.

At 10.00am, Dr Galpin convened an inquest in the prison at which Governor Brown was required to confirm Bailey's details and that sentence of death had been passed in the manner required by law.

'And I think I am correct in saying,' Galpin asked Brown, 'that the sentence was carried out expeditiously, and to your entire satisfaction?'

'Yes, and most humanely,' came the reply.

Dr Sankey, the prison's Medical Officer, merely corroborated Brown's evidence, adding 'skilfully' to the assessment of Ellis's methods and 'instantaneous' to the moment of Bailey's death. The jury returned a verdict to the effect that death was carried out in accordance with the law.

The prison records required that there be an official assessment by Brown and Sankey of the work carried out by Ellis and Taylor.

Opinion of the Governer [sic] *and Medical Officer as to the Mannor* [sic] *of the above named persons has performed his duty.*

1. Has he performed his duty well?

Yes Yes

2. Was his general demeanour satisfactory during the period he was in the Prison, and does he appear to be a respectable person?

Yes Yes

3. Has he shown capacity both physical and mental for the duty, and suitability for the post?

Yes yes

4. Is there any ground for supposing he will bring discredit upon his office by lecturing, or granting interviews to persons who may wish to elicit information from him in regard to the execution or any other act?

No No

5. Are you aware of any circumstances before, at or after the execution that will tend to show that he is not a suitable person to employ on future occasions either on account of incapacity for performing the duty, or the likely hood [sic] of him creating a public scandal before, on or after an execution?

No No

The following day, Mr Parrott, the Under-Sheriff, a respected Aylesbury solicitor by profession, sent a note to the Under-Secretary of State at the Home Office: 'I beg to inform you that George Arthur Bailey was duly executed at HM Prison Oxford yesterday and that John Ellis of 3 Kitchen Lane, Balderstone Fold, Rochdale, who was employed as executioner, carried out his duties satisfactorily.'

Ellis was paid his usual £10 fee, while Taylor received two guineas. Both were also allowed reasonable expenses including third-class rail fares.

By the time the Home Office received official notification of his death, Bailey had been buried, as tradition had it, within the precincts of the prison; he was just short of his 33rd birthday. The current Oxfordshire Archives record Bailey as being consigned to plot 11, between 'J Rose', who was interred on 19 February 1919, and 'HD Seymour', who was buried on 10 December 1931.

In the month-and-a-half between his trial at Aylesbury and the hangman's noose, Bailey had spent much of his time in prison writing poetry. These two pieces, with their odd misspellings and even the occasional invented word, might give some indication of his state of mind during those final weeks:

Knowledge of thy love directs my way, thy will
Inspiring men to calm in thine own way. Yet still —
The doubts that I am a coward saddens me;
The truth so hard to bear; cursed sympathy.
Your broken heart. Oh God, my senses reel.
How can I swear the truth to save my hurt,
O Kit, that I could join thee, 'neath mother earth.
Lassie, our babe, in God's hands we must save;
Lest this be our sacrifice — bab's way to pave.
Your love, my sacrifice, shriven souls, bab's worth.
Revelling in my blindness, bloated pride; falsering.
O girlie, yet my love had never died; it brings
Nearer to me thy spirit's sweet comunionship — unsmirched

Restless, yet patient, waiting, ah —
When will that glad call come?
Weary, heartsore, the goal yet afar.
When will my life's work be done?
When God wills it, loved one, and not
At my wish
When God's way is won, dear, sun shining
Through mist.
Then will the call find me waiting for thee.
Then will you hasten to me.

So, finally joined in death barely five months after the dreadful events of late September, the murderer and his victim, husband and wife, also now shared the prospect of eternity in unmarked graves.

12

THE JUDGE AND
THE HANGMAN

With suicide becoming such a recurring motif throughout Bailey's life and trial, it is strange – arguably, beyond strange to the point of almost bizarre coincidence – that, within the space of six months, between 20 September 1932 and 26 April 1933 – barely ten years after they had shared in the fate of the Musical Milkman – John Ellis and Sir Henry McCardie committed suicide themselves in their own homes in perhaps equally sad and, in the case of Ellis especially, exceedingly grisly circumstances. They were, respectively, 58 and 63 years of age.

Ellis's career as an executioner lasted more than 20 years. In total, he had hanged 203 people, including six Sinn Feiners before breakfast one day in Dublin during the First World War – two at 6.00am, two at 7.00am and two at 8.00am. And among many notorious others, he was the dispatcher of Dr

Crippen, George 'the Brides in the Bath' Smith, Sir Roger Casement and Major Herbert Armstrong. Sadly for Ellis, he had tried to take his own life on more than one occasion following his retirement in 1923.

Eight months after his final execution – of John Eastwood at Leeds Prison at the end of that December – Ellis was discovered by his wife Annie, sitting in a chair at their home in Rochdale with a bullet wound in his jaw. He was taken to hospital and then, two days later, after being discharged, straight to the local Magistrates' Court where he was charged with attempting to commit suicide.

Before a packed court with, it is reported, hundreds of others turned away, a dishevelled and clearly distraught Ellis admitted the charge, telling the Chairman of the Magistrates that he could give no reason for the attempt before promising him faithfully that he would not try again.

The Chairman replied, 'I am very sorry to see you here, Ellis. If your aim had been as straight as the "drops" you have given, it would have been a bad job for you. Your life has been lengthened and I hope you will make the best use of it – the spare life which has been granted to you,' adding, and here was the crux of the matter, 'My colleagues want me to say that in your own interests, as well as the interests of your wife, it would be advisable for you to give up the drink. I hope that you will be able to give that promise, as the drink has led you to this.'

This second promise given, Ellis was duly discharged after being bound over for 12 months.

So how had it come to this quite so soon after Ellis had stepped down following a long and generally distinguished reign as an acknowledged master of the noose? It may have had something to do with the fact that Ellis – once described as 'the coolest, most self-possessed executioner ever known' – had a particular aversion to hanging women. The law, of course, made no such distinction, and the memories of these duties took the greatest toll on this normally mild-mannered man who was a barber by profession.

During his career, he was involved in the execution of just three women: in 1903, as an assistant in the hanging of Emily Swann for the murder of her husband; in October 1923, Susan Newell for killing a 12-year-old schoolboy; and, earlier that same year, Edith Thompson for inciting her 'toy boy' lover Frederick Bywaters to the fatal stabbing of her husband Percy Thompson, her guilt seemingly established through a series of passionate love letters.

The case was a sensation in its day, a tabloid feeding frenzy, with Bywaters protesting Thompson's innocence to the very end, while the flirty Thompson did herself no favours by insisting on giving evidence against the advice of her Counsel. But no sooner had a very sensationalist media coverage of their Old Bailey trial ceased after both were sentenced to hang than the papers suddenly seemed to shift their position. They were moved, it seemed, by Bywaters' unwavering loyalty to the attractive Thompson who might have been, on reflection, more silly than scarlet, and the fact that no woman had hanged in Britain for more than 15 years. This dramatic lurch in public attitude was reflected in a petition against both executions signed by more than a million people. 'If these two are hanged, judge and jury are murderers also' was now a typical reaction.

It was into this hothouse atmosphere that Ellis stepped after being invited by the Under-Sheriff of Essex, Mr Gepp, to hang Bywaters and Thompson. Ellis accepted, still thinking that Thompson, at least, would most likely be reprieved. When, a week or so later, they both had their appeals dismissed, Ellis was then asked by Gepp if he'd take care of just Thompson as it was likely the pair would be hanged on the same day at, of course, separate prisons, thus requiring two executioners.

In his memoirs, which begin, tellingly, with a chapter entitled 'Edith Thompson: How I Hanged a Woman', Ellis wrote that he was 'troubled for hours' before deciding to accept then, having accepted, 'guessed the general public would regard me as a morbid, depraved monster, and I wasn't long left in any doubt about that'. All kinds of hate mail flooded in from a fickle public who had undergone a complete *volte-face* in such a short period of time. Ellis tried to console himself with the fact that he also got plenty of letters from men 'in every station of life who hankered for the hangman's job'.

History relates that, on the morning of her execution, Thompson moved, within the last hour of her life, from total composure to, in the very final minutes, a state of complete collapse and had literally to be carried to the scaffold. Ellis, who said that her 'cries and semi-demented body movements all but unnerved me', then, intriguingly, describes her dying 'instantaneously and painlessly'. What he signally doesn't mention in his own account of her ghastly end was that, as the trapdoor opened, the sudden impact of the noose caused her to haemorrhage massively in the lower abdomen. After this, women facing execution were required to wear special canvas undergarments to prevent – or perhaps one should say, better disguise – a recurrence of Thompson's copious bleeding.

Thompson's execution at Holloway, followed just four months later by Susan Newell's in Glasgow – the first woman to be executed in that city for 70 years – clearly hastened

Ellis's retirement after 23 years in his unconventional, part-time profession, although he would always claim that their respective dispatch had no lasting effect on him.

It's rather ironic that the Chairman of the Rochdale Magistrates in Ellis's home town, where he had grown up before following into his father's hairdressing business, made such a business of 'the drink' in those admonitory closing remarks, as it had been just that which had given rise to an extraordinary event much earlier in Ellis's career. In July 1910, while an assistant to Henry Pierrepoint, first of that famous family – followed by brother Thomas then son Albert into the execution profession – the pair got into a fight while preparing a day before the hanging of Frederick Foreman at Chelmsford Prison.

As the warders were handing over the prisoner's details to the hangmen, it seems Pierrepoint started shouting at Ellis after the latter, the older man by four years, had advised him to drink less as it 'gave the public the impression he had to drink to do his work'. Then, Ellis would write later: 'He rushed at me and knocked me off the chair I was sat on. I got up but was again knocked off. He was going for me again when warder Nash, who had heard the noise, came in and attempted to stop him, but failed, and the blow struck me behind the ear.'

After this, Henry Pierrepoint was removed from the list of approved executioners. The official version at the time was that he'd resigned. Years later, files released from the Public Record office indicated that he'd been sacked after arriving at Chelmsford 'considerably the worse for drink'.

Ellis's own drinking appears not to have been even remotely a problem until after he retired and he was back hairdressing and breeding dogs, albeit something of a tourist attraction in his native Rochdale. But, following his brush with death, things went from weird to worse. Unable to settle down to a regular job, he looked for any distraction, including taking the part of the hangman in a play about the 19th-century cat burglar and killer, Charlie Peace, whom he had to 'execute' on stage. The production caused a furore in the press and questions in the Commons, so after just a week's run it was taken off.

Having kept the scaffold from the play, Ellis, by now drinking heavily and with his business suffering badly, next became a sort of music hall act touring towns and fairs giving demonstrations of his exotic ex-craft until, on the eve of taking his road show to London, he became so ill and depressed he had to abandon it and returned home.

On the evening of 20 September 1932, after enjoying a cup of tea with his wife and daughter Amy, suddenly and without warning he grabbed a cut-throat razor and threatened them that he'd cut off their heads. Terrified, they rushed outside and to the nearby house of Ellis's oldest son, Austin. Austin quickly returned to the family home only in time to see his father slash his own throat with the razor.

When the police arrived, Ellis was by now lying in a pool of blood with 5in-long gashes to the throat. 'It struck me he had suddenly gone mad,' said wife Annie at the inquest, having also told the Coroner that her husband had suffered from neuritis, heart trouble and nerves. Recording a verdict of suicide, he said, 'I am quite of the opinion that he did this rash act in a sudden frenzy of madness.'

In one of the newspaper reports of his death, Ellis was described by the *Rochdale Observer* as 'having a pale complexion with hair thinning on top and a heavy, sandy moustache', and it added that he was a man who had prided himself on getting all the details of his grim work correct and as streamlined as possible. They also quoted Ellis from a past interview, saying, 'People do not realise the jeers and insults with which hangmen have to put up. In company, some people get up and won't stay in the same room with you.'

The shadow of his job clearly hung, and would continue to do so until his dreadful death, very heavy indeed.

★ ★ ★

'BACHELOR JUDGE' SHOT DEAD
MR JUSTICE MCCARDIE FOUND CLASPING GUN
TRAGEDY IN HIS LIBRARY — MAID HEARS FATAL SHOT
STRING IN HIS HAND

This sensational four-tier, front-page headline in the *Daily Mirror* of 27 April 1933 could barely contain its prurient excitement reporting the death of the 'celebrity' judge with an oddly ambivalent nickname at his fashionable service flat in Queen Anne's Mansions, St James's — a suite of rooms on the fourth floor overlooking the park. 'A member of staff,' the newspaper continued breathlessly in two paragraphs of solid bold type, 'while approaching the flat door, heard a shot and, rushing into the room, found Sir Henry on the floor unconscious. A shotgun was between his knees. The *Daily Mirror* understands that attached to the trigger of the gun was a piece of string, the other end of which was held by the Judge's right hand.'

The broadsheets were all but drooling, too, as they described how Sir Henry was found — note a slightly differing account — 'seated in a crumpled position in a chair and bleeding from a wound under the chin'. The weapon, for them, was 'a sporting rifle' rather than a mere 'shotgun', more consistent with a grandee who listed, a little ironically considering his demise, two of his hobbies in *Who's Who* as 'shooting and fishing'.

The workaholic Judge, always a controversial figure who seemed to provoke affection and criticism equally during his 17 years on the Bench, was known in the months before his death to have suffered from a debilitating bout of 'flu which in turn led to lack of sleep and, according to his friends, 'fits of depression and weakness'. Not long before he died, the other residents and staff at Queen Anne's Mansions would remark they had found him 'more reserved than usual and obviously depressed at times'. Even his beloved walks in St James's Park had become much less frequent.

What did become clear straight away after he died was that he had found life on the circuit outside London increasingly vexing. 'I feel I am cut off from London,' he was reported as saying. 'London is the one place to live in. Some of my brother Judges like the quiet of these provincial towns and the Judge's lodgings in them. But I feel that I am exiled from London. There are few interesting people one meets on circuit. Exile ... I dine alone or I dine at a public function. There is an art in living. One can get the best out of life if one knows how to live properly.' If only one could, he might have added, clearly homesick for his elegant rooms in London, SW1.

Was there possibly a clue to his state of mind in the caption of one of the two photographs on the *Daily Mirror*'s front page? The main picture showed the Judge fully robed striding out with purpose; the second featured him in civvies relaxing with friends at a race meeting. It was only after his death that a story began circulating that Sir Henry had incurred massive gambling debts and was allegedly being blackmailed.

Despite a hankering for his adopted capital, McCardie, who'd been one of the youngest men ever appointed a Judge at the comparatively early age of 47, had roots that were far from London and hardly typical of the traditional, upper-middle-class public school template for advancement in the judiciary. His father had emigrated from County Derry during the Irish Potato Famine to Birmingham, where he set up a button-making business, but died when Sir Henry, one of six siblings, was only eight.

Said to have been intelligent but lazy, he left school at 16 and worked for several years in an auctioneer's office before being called to the Bar in 1894. Despite the lack of a university degree and family 'connections', his progress on the Midlands and Oxford Circuit was rapid, probably due to his voracious appetite for work. On just one day, legend has it, he once handled 21 different cases in 21 different courts. The light in his chambers used to burn so long and so hard, the place became known as 'the lighthouse'.

Such a workload inevitably yielded its financial reward and, even as a junior barrister, he was earning £20,000 a year, a staggering sum for that time. The next step was obviously to 'apply for silk', to become a King's Counsel but, for whatever reason, there was an inordinate delay in the Lord Chancellor's office, so much so that McCardie decided to withdraw his application because it was proving a distraction to his day-to-day business. His elevation to High Court Judge only six years later – apparently on the nod of the then Prime Minister Herbert Asquith, who'd been a distinguished lawyer before entering politics – was especially remarkable considering not only his age but also, perhaps as significantly, how few had previously attained the office without a prestigious KC or QC.

McCardie's appointment came about when Sir Edward Scrutton ascended to 'Lord Justice Scrutton', the latest recruit to the Court of Appeal, and the two men's lives would intersect again on more than one occasion in a much less agreeable fashion, most famously the year before McCardie killed himself. This was in a sequel to what had become known as 'The Helen of Troy' case – originally before McCardie in Cambridge – in which an action had been brought by a husband for damages for enticement from him of his wife. On appeal, the Court of Appeal ordered a re-trial, which was presided over by a fresh Judge, and the judgment – this time for the plaintiff – was reversed.

Lord Scrutton, in his Court's consideration of the Cambridge hearing, mounted an unveiled attack on McCardie, one which would only go to compound the 'Bachelor Judge' epithet. He stated, 'If there is to be a discussion of the relations of husbands and wives, I think it would come better from Judges who had more than theoretical knowledge of husbands and wives. I am a little surprised that a gentleman who has never been married should proceed to explain the proper underclothing that ladies should wear.' The unexplained antipathy between the two men – one stuffy and deeply academic, the other popular if occasionally, unwisely, mercurial – would even, at one embarrassing juncture, result in them shouting at each other in open Court.

McCardie – who once said, 'a bachelor is a man who looks before he leaps and having leaped does not look at all' – certainly didn't let his single status prevent him from pontificating long and often on the subject of women and their supposed wants in various cases down the years. His *Times* obituary couldn't resist quoting from one of his more outspoken judgments in relation to a husband's obligation to pay his wife's dress bills.

'Her catholicity of profusion was remarkable. She threw herself beneath the fatal curse of luxury. She forgot that those who possess substantial means are trustees to use them with prudence, charity and propriety. She forgot that ostentation is the worst form of vulgarity. She ignored the sharp menace of future penury. Dress, and dress alone, seems to have been her end in life. She sought felicity in the ceaseless changes of trivial fashions.'

His withering indictment of the thrice-married Mrs Nash didn't end there. A closer look at his 1923 judgment in the case of Callot and Others v Nash, further reveals, 'Self-decoration was her vision, her aim, her creed. I observe no record of any act of beneficence, not a trace of unselfish aid to others; she computed her enjoyment of life by the reckless indulgence of her extravagance. Well was it said by Mr Hazlitt, in one of his essays: "Those who make their dress the principal part of themselves will, in general, become of no more value than their dress."'

Even the *Daily Mirror* felt moved to reproduce what they described as various nuggets of previous 'McCardie Wisdom': 'The dress of women has been ever the mystery, and sometimes the calamity, of the ages ...'; 'I believe two-thirds of the money spent by women on dress is spent without necessity ...'; 'Too many women are the slaves of fashion and too many men are the slaves of women ...'; 'The perils of a husband do not grow less as the years go by ...'

Women and their preoccupations – which also included, variously, pronouncements on abortion (he supported legalisation), sterilisation and birth control – weren't the only matters on which McCardie stirred controversy in a career across many branches of the law. There was, for example, a libel action brought by a former Lieutenant Governor of the Punjab, Sir Michael O'Dwyer, against an Indian politician who'd asserted in a 1924 publication that O'Dwyer was responsible for the Amritsar Massacre in 1919, during which an unarmed native throng in the Punjabi city were fired on by troops led by General 'The Butcher of Amritsar' Dyer, resulting in nearly 400 deaths – probably a conservative estimate – and many more casualties. Dyer, whose actions were condoned by O'Dwyer, was later relieved of his command and not re-employed. In his judgment, McCardie not only remarked that Dyer had 'acted rightly' but also 'in my opinion, was wrongly punished by the Secretary of State for India'.

McCardie's sporadic, left-field statements probably account for the fact that the Courts over which he presided were more often than not packed. As barrister Albert Crew noted in the 1932 compilation *Judicial Wisdom of Mr Justice McCardie*, a surprisingly readable collection of his cases and judgments spanning everything from 'Domestic and Social Relations' to 'Divorce Cases' and 'Other Legal Cases of General Interest', but no murders: 'Certainly, since Lord Darling [High Court Judge, Charles, Baron Darling] retired, there has been no other Judge whose Court the average student or junior practitioner, anxious to learn the tricks of his trade, selects so readily to pass an idle hour.'

Then, a little over a year after he had donned the black cap for Bailey, he presided at the Old Bailey in almost back-to-back trials for murders committed within just a few days of each other, cases which aroused considerable public feeling.

On 6 March 1922, Ronald True, public school-educated and an invalided-out Royal Flying Corps veteran murdered a prostitute in Fulham. His Defence tried to establish insanity but he was found guilty and sentenced to death.

On 14 March, Henry Jacoby, an 18-year-old pantry boy, battered 65-year-old Lady White with a hammer in her London hotel room after panicking during a mission to steal from guests' bedrooms. In the latter, McCardie advised the jury that if the blows were struck to inflict grievous bodily harm, and the victim died as a result, then the assailant would be guilty of murder. Jacoby was duly found guilty but there was a recommendation of mercy from the jury on account of his youth.

Both men were due to be hanged by John Ellis, who in his memoirs said he confidently expected the Home Secretary to take account of the jury's recommendation while noting his own personal feeling that he hoped there would be a reprieve for a boy who many believed should have been charged with manslaughter rather than murder. No such mercy was given and Jacoby was hanged. Two days after Ellis returned to Rochdale, he received official notification that he wouldn't be required to hang True as the 30-year-old fantasist, apparently from a wealthy background, had been granted a reprieve on the grounds of insanity. A public debate then inevitably ensued over what was perceived as two kinds of justice – one for the rich and one for the poor – with the implication that McCardie was somehow complicit.

A decade later, and barely six months after Ellis had slashed his own throat in a fit of depression, Sir Henry McCardie was also dead violently by his own hand, his mind probably as disturbed as Ellis's. Their parallel lives in administering the law had crossed in the most unlikely fashion for the final time.

However, it doesn't quite end there. In a fascinating if chilling footnote to the tale of the Judge and the hangman, there must also be, more briefly, recalled a third and, arguably as significant, addition to this bizarre roll-call of suicide, which is inextricably linked to the Musical Milkman Murder case. It involves that of perhaps the Prosecution's most high-profile witness, the legendary Sir Bernard Spilsbury, often described as 'the father of modern forensics'.

By the time he gassed himself to death aged 70 in his own laboratory at University College, London, shortly before Christmas 1947, Spilsbury had, in a career lasting more than 40 years, completed over 20,000 autopsies and spoken for the Prosecution at some 200 trials, of which only a few resulted in acquittal. It was said that he only had to turn up at a mortuary for an accused man to be condemned.

An exhaustive but often highly critical 2007 biography, Lethal Witness by Andrew Rose, suggests that the ultra-conservative Spilsbury was distinctly over-celebrated. It is proposed that the man who worked alone and considered himself infallible may even have been responsible through a combination of his methods, personal agenda – he was homophobic and anti-abortion – and confident, dare-defy-me, Court delivery for several miscarriages of justice, including Crippen. Even by the 1930s, his expertise was beginning to be questioned.

A 50-cigarettes-a-day smoker, apparently to help counter the smell of death in his lab, Spilsbury was, by 1947, a broken man, estranged from his wife, devastated by the death of two of his sons – one in the Blitz, another of TB – and depressed that his own powers were all but broken by the onset of dementia and severe arthritis. His lonely demise, achieved from the open tap of a Bunsen burner, may have been prompted by the fear of losing his pre-eminence or, even possibly, from a belated sense of guilt that he was at least partly responsible for hastening several innocents to the scaffold.

The untimely deaths by their own hand of McCardie, Ellis and Spilsbury might suggest that George Arthur Bailey had the very last laugh.

EPILOGUE

Hollie celebrated – if that's the right word – her third birthday on 10 October 1920, four days after her mother was buried in Little Marlow Cemetery. Her father, whom she saw for the very last time a week earlier, the day he'd bundled his little daughter on to the train to take her to Jim and Helen Jennings' house in Swindon, was now on remand in Oxford Prison ahead of various preliminary hearings, the trial and his eventual execution a little over four months later.

She wasn't destined to stay long at Aunt Helen's because, for whatever reason, and it would perhaps become a bit clearer many years later, her grandmother Betsy travelled up to Wiltshire to collect her on the very day Hollie was due to be handed over to Dr Barnardo's, the children's charity. The charity's first orphanage in London's East End had been opened exactly 50 years earlier by Irish-born philanthropist Thomas John Barnardo.

Betsy, a widow for 15 years since her husband Thomas had died of 'acute melancholia' in the workhouse, eventually moved from West Hampstead to live in a pretty little cottage at Berrynarbor, near Hele Bay on the north Devon coast, less than six miles from where she had been born and raised. Unable to attend her son's trial because of illness, she at least now stepped in to give Hollie something approximating a family home.

'My grandmother, she was a real tartar, a real Victorian,' Hollie told Bob Perrin when she visited Little Marlow in 1984. 'She was the sort you never asked questions. Actually she never showed me any affection, never even kissed me,' she also recalled wistfully.

Having first been fobbed off with 'your parents died of the fever' – probably a reference to the post Great War 'flu epidemic – as the years passed, Hollie said she heard 'the occasional snatch of adult conversation which hinted at a much darker secret'. Presumably, that botched 'triple suicide' – though the death of a then two-year-old would have been difficult to be explained away as 'suicide' – as alluded to in the letter to my father in 1974. She was always, however, too afraid to ask.

There were, she did vividly remember, 'recurring nightmares. I'd be clawing at a mound of earth because I knew a body was underneath. But I'd always stop before uncovering the body because I woke up thinking that I'd murdered someone. Of course, I hadn't. I presume there was something in my subconscious, something that came from lying next to my dead mother when she was wrapped in a sheet. I don't know.'

It was a 'strict, religious upbringing', a member of Hollie's surviving family told me, but 'on the whole, quite a happy one', said another, and Hollie had become a Sunday School teacher at 17.

At some point after 1920, the pair moved to the very opposite end of the county, to the tiny village of Starcross on the Exe estuary in South Devon. In 1935, Hollie held her grandmother's hand for the last time after nursing her through her final illness.

With nothing now to keep her in this rural backwater, Hollie decided to try her luck again with Aunt Helen, who was still living in Swindon. But it seems that the remembrance of terrible things past still weighed very heavily with Bailey's sister. Hollie recalled her grandmother's will being torn up in front of her by Helen who said bitterly, 'We don't want to know about that.'

It quickly became clear that there was no home for Hollie at the Jennings' who, after all, must have arranged for her to be bundled off to Barnardo's with almost indecent haste all those years earlier.

From the mid-1930s, Hollie went 'into service' as a children's nanny, first for a couple of families then, later, at a private school where she worked for the people who owned the place. In 1939, she married her first husband, an employee at a local electrical company, before he joined up with the Royal Engineers during the Second World War. He was killed at Salerno following the Allied invasion of Italy in September 1943.

Hollie was married four times, the last in 1985. Widowed twice – to husbands one and four, and divorced twice, to two and three, she had five children, as well as, subsequently, flocks of grandchildren and great-grandchildren.

Alongside the stirring up of memories from her own childhood, the 1984 visit also brought back another tragic reminder: the suicide four years earlier of an 18-year-old granddaughter after, she said, a row with her father.

'Have I the Mark of Cain on me?' she exclaimed to Bob Perrin. 'To me, he [Bailey] was a madman – so what have I passed on to my family? What have I given to my children, to their generation? It makes me feel guilty, which I shouldn't, but I do.'

Of her father, she continued, 'I don't know if I am doing him an injustice, but I feel very bitter about him. He robbed me of my mother … I've no feeling for him. He deprived me of a happy, normal home life. I don't know what my mother was or what she did but, certainly, she didn't deserve to die like that … But why? Always the question why? And then with the girl [Miss Marks] in the next bedroom … what sort of feelings could he have had? No, I've no feelings for him. She must have been in agony …'

Yet she still felt compelled to pass on a few other recollections, of more 'human' moments, involving experiences with her father.

'I remember going out on his milk float. It was night because he'd lit the lights on the side of the float. Coming back, presumably from Bourne End, he took a wrong turning and had to turn back the horse. I remember him tucking a rug around my knees. The other memory is of him pushing me down the steps of Swindon railway station in my pushchair. That must have been the day after he'd murdered my mother. He was taking me to his sister's. I remember he wore a gabardine mac with some sort of trilby. But I can't see his face. I just can't see his face.'

After she had walked all round the cottage inside and out

– 'I think my mother made me happy here' – Hollie headed next for the cemetery for another look at her mother's bleak, unmarked grave. And despite the curate having, ten years earlier, told her it would be difficult to find because the numbers had been 'lost or misplaced', it was, in fact, still perfectly locatable on the official parish record.

As she gazed mournfully at Plot 256, Hollie said, 'I've no recollection of her [Kate] at all. I seem to remember walking down a country lane with someone and a little kitten was following us. But was that my mother or my grandmother? I don't know.'

Then, later, as she left the hallowed ground, Hollie suddenly said, according to the report in the *Bucks Free Press*, 'It's my dear wish to be buried beside her.'

Twenty years later, Hollie, now 86, was at her local supermarket in the West Country town where she'd lived since the late 1930s, when she was targeted by two young East European women. One distracted her while the other made off with her handbag containing a large sum of cash. The effect was devastating to the elderly woman. She would go back to the store constantly to see if she could spot her muggers. Her health, which had been generally good all her life, aside from the occasional bout of depression, deteriorated rapidly following the attack.

She died seven months later, her death certificate indicating, among other things, kidney failure 'secondary to hypertension'. That same document also, intriguingly, registered Hollie's place of birth as, not the Infirmary at Winchester Prison, but 'Little Marlow, Buckinghamshire'. So, although finally laid to rest in the West Country – after cremation her ashes were buried next to those of a dead son – perhaps the spirit at least of that final plea as Hollie left the cemetery in 1984 was somehow partially fulfilled.

One of her children told me, 'All her life she was looking for answers. Even finding out what happened didn't really give her the answers she needed.'

Hollie's favourite song was, poignantly, the Coben/Foree standard, 'Nobody's Child', about the trials and tribulations of an orphan, which was first recorded by Hank Snow in 1949 before being 'covered' endlessly by everyone from Lonnie Donegan and Hank Williams Jr to The Beatles and The Traveling Wilburys. It was played at her funeral in 2004.

APPENDIX I
A MODERN LAWYER'S VIEW

Brian Lett QC is a criminal barrister with over 40 years' experience of the Courts of England and Wales. He has also sat for many years as a part-time Criminal Judge. Brian's expertise in the criminal law is internationally recognised, and he has taken part in training seminars for Criminal Judges in the Eastern Caribbean and Northern Cyprus, on behalf of the United Kingdom and the European Union.

The trial of Bailey would have been very different today. Our criminal law and procedure have changed significantly over the last 90 years. The death penalty is long gone, and there is perhaps a greater understanding today of the various shades of guilt that may arise from a defendant's mental state.

No longer does the law impose such a strict and clear-cut distinction between 'mad' and 'bad', and the law now provides a defendant with a number of ways in which he may avoid conviction for the offence of murder, while still being culpable of the unlawful killing of another.

But would the result of the trial have been different? Bailey would no longer have been executed, but would a jury have convicted him of murder?

What has not changed much or at all is human nature. Thus, the human beings who comprise our juries today experience many of the same feelings, and perhaps suffer from some of the same prejudices, as the jury who tried Bailey. The crimes that juries try today, when stripped of modern gadgetry, weapons and drug abuse, are not so very different from those that have been tried by juries for centuries.

Tiring of a wife, and lusting after other young women in her place, is a time-honoured failing of a married man, although only the very few turn to murder to achieve the fulfilment of their desires. Thus, the thrust of the Prosecution case against Bailey would not be very different from many cases tried by a jury today.

In modern times, the fact that a guilty verdict might well lead to the execution of a defendant might well deter some jurors from convicting. In contrast, the climate in 1921, even with female jurors serving on juries for the first time, was very different. The Great War, with its millions of blameless deaths, was very recent history. Most, if not all, jurors would have lost a member of their family or a close friend in that conflict. The fact that, if they convicted a bad man of murder, his life would be forfeit would not have troubled them unduly.

In modern terms, it seems remarkable that the Bailey jury convicted of capital murder after a retirement of only 30 minutes. That would not happen today. Reading through the transcript, I felt very sorry for Defence Counsel, Mr Johnston, who, with his client's life resting in his hands, made a closing address of three-and-a-half hours – seven times as long as the jury's retirement.

However, the court procedure was significantly different in those days. The Prosecution always had the first word [as they still do today] and the last word [this now belongs to the Defence]. The very experienced Mr Hugo Young KC took 1 hour and 20 minutes in his closing speech to demolish the arguments that Johnston had so painstakingly put forward in his lengthy address.

Mr Young KC's closing speech was then followed by a rather hostile summing up from the Judge. The jury retired with the words of the Judge and prosecuting Counsel, not the Defence, ringing most recently in their ears.

The Judge described the four-day trial as a long trial, which would certainly not be the case today, when Crown Court trials frequently last for weeks or months. However, the Court in the Bailey trial worked very long hours. The trial took place in January, when daylight was short, and the Court sat on Thursday, Friday, Saturday [when they eventually rose at 6.50pm] and on Monday.

The final day started at 10.30am. Johnston, for the Defence, called a final witness, and then addressed the jury. His speech could not have finished much earlier than 2.30pm, or later if it was interrupted by lunch.

Allowing for an hour's lunch, and for Mr Young KC's closing speech, the Judge probably did not start summing up until after 5.00pm. His summing up took 1 hour and 10 minutes.

If the jury did not retire until perhaps 6.30pm, then perhaps it is not so surprising that they reached their verdict as quickly as they did. If they felt that the issue was clear, and the verdict obvious, they would not waste time on unnecessary discussion.

Further, following the practice of the time, the jury had been confined together throughout the trial. They were not allowed to go home at night, and remained under confinement throughout the Sunday rest day. Thus, by Monday evening, they were no doubt keen to get home to their loved ones.

In contrast, the jury of today will normally start its working day at 10.00–10.30am, will take an hour for lunch, and will rarely finish later than 4.30pm [when the air conditioning switches off in certain courts!]. After their day's work, they will be sent home.

Even if they are in retirement considering their verdict, they will nonetheless be told to break off, and will be sent home for the night not long after 4.00pm. It is fair to say, of course, that the working day has shrunk considerably in modern Britain. In the 1920s, most people worked a five-and-a-half- or six-day week, and the working day would for many start at dawn, and finish at dusk.

But would this have made a difference to the verdict?

In 1921, the law of murder was clear and emphatic. To prove the offence of murder, the Crown had to prove against the defendant that he or she unlawfully killed another person and that, at the time of doing so, intended to cause the victim really serious bodily harm or death. What lawyers call the 'actus reus' – the act of unlawful killing – had to be proved beyond reasonable doubt, as did the 'mens rea' – that the defendant at the time of the killing had the necessary intention to kill or do really serious bodily harm.

Bailey could not claim that the killing of his wife was

lawful, even if it had come about by her own hand. Suicide was then unlawful, and, if he helped his wife to kill herself, it would be murder.

Mr Justice Avory, when he delivered the judgment of the Court of Appeal dismissing Bailey's appeal, put the law succinctly: 'The law is that if persons agree to commit suicide, and one survives, the one who survived will be guilty of murder. And if two persons agree to take poison, and one backs out of it, then again, the survivor is guilty of murder.'

Today, Bailey would not have faced that problem. The law has changed. The Homicide Act 1957 reduced murder to manslaughter [not a capital crime] where a person can prove, on balance, that the killing to which he was a party was a part of a suicide pact. Four years later, the Suicide Act 1961 abrogated the long-standing common law rule that suicide was a crime – thus, neither suicide nor attempted suicide is now a crime. However, aiding and abetting suicide remains at the present time a crime punishable by up to 14 years' imprisonment.

Insanity was and remains a defence to murder and all other crimes. The legal criteria by which insanity is to be judged are found in what are called the M'Naghten Rules, dating from 1843. In short, as the trial Judge directed the jury, and as Mr Justice Avory repeated in the Court of Appeal judgment, the defence of insanity can only succeed if a defendant proves, on balance, that, at the time of committing the act, he was labouring under such a defect of reason, from a disease of the mind, that he did not know the nature and quality of the act he was doing; or, if he did know it, that he did not know what he was doing was wrong.

However, the results of a successful defence of insanity in a murder case are unattractive for the accused, since he will be confined to a mental hospital indefinitely, although at least, before the abolition of capital punishment, he would not be executed.

The only medical report upon Bailey's mental state that the Court received came from the Prison Medical Officer, Dr RH Sankey [presumably not a qualified psychiatrist]. His short report concluded that he did not consider Bailey to be certifiable as insane, and that he was fit to plead [fitness to plead meaning that he could properly understand the court proceedings, give evidence and give instructions to his legal team]. Although Dr Sankey's report appears not to have been presented to the jury, Mr Johnston had little with which he could contradict it. Certainly, in relation to fitness to plead, Bailey was clearly able to follow the proceedings, give instructions and give evidence.

Mr Young KC, in his opening speech for the Prosecution, told the jury that, although no defence had been declared in advance [unlike today, when this is normally done by way of a Defence Case Statement], he thought it possible that the Defence would raise the question of the defendant's state of mind. He dismissed that approach, saying that, although the defendant was a peculiar man in some respects, he knew what he was doing.

Mr Johnston, defending, appears to have been confused and far from specific in relation to the question of insanity, and to have changed his approach during the course of Bailey's defence. It seems that his client did not want him to run such a defence and, in the end, he did not do so.

In cross-examination of the Prosecution witnesses, Mr Johnston clearly raised the issue and, in his opening speech for the Defence, according to the *Bucks Free Press*, he 'implored the jury, instead of coming to the conclusion that [Bailey] was the greatest villain that they had ever heard or seen, to decide that he was mad'. Perhaps Mr Johnston initially hoped to run this line of defence in tandem with Bailey's own defence that on the facts that he had not committed the crime.

However, after Bailey had given evidence, and called witnesses, Mr Johnston abandoned the question of insanity, telling the jury that he 'was not going to advance that point, but to build up the Defence on the grounds that the prisoner was in no way responsible for his wife's death'.

Mr Young KC, in his closing speech for the Crown, having declared that, since the Defence were not advancing the question of insanity, it was not necessary for him to 'say another word on that point', then proceeded to take some time scathingly to dismiss the various points raised in the evidence suggestive of some sort of mental illness.

The trial Judge, fairly, left the issue open to the jury, but they would not have wasted any time on it. The Defence had not proved that the defendant was insane, and the defendant had given evidence coherently and at some length before them.

The fact that Bailey might be odd, eccentric or unusual was nowhere near enough. To be insane, he would have to prove that at the time of the killing of his wife he was suffering from a disease of the mind that meant that he did not know the nature or quality of his acts, or that they were wrong. Bailey could not begin to do that.

Today, an alternative line of defence is available. Like insanity, it may avoid conviction for murder and thus [if it still existed] the death penalty. It is that of 'diminished responsibility', a concept introduced to our law by Section 2 of the Homicide Act 1957.

A defendant who successfully runs the defence of

diminished responsibility will still be convicted of manslaughter [unlawful killing but without the intention to kill or do really serious bodily harm], but will be acquitted of murder, and thus, in 1957, would not be in danger of execution.

Diminished responsibility is defined as an abnormality of mind such as substantially impairs an accused's mental responsibility for his act. It is a defence to murder often advanced by psychopaths, who kill without any concept of fault. If it succeeds, it may well lead to exactly the same sentence of life imprisonment as for murder, but the conviction will be for manslaughter. In days gone by, it was a means of avoiding execution.

A colourful illustration of what is meant by diminished responsibility is the following story, regularly used by barristers to juries: 'Two men are walking along a river bank. The river is known to contain a man-eating crocodile. One man deliberately pushes the other into the river, with the intention that the crocodile will eat him. The crocodile duly does so. The man who pushed his companion into the river is guilty of murder. However, the crocodile is guilty only of manslaughter, because his responsibility is diminished. He eats people because that is what he does. He is a crocodile. He has no concept of fault. He sees nothing wrong in eating people.'

Thus, the law today is significantly different to that which was in force in 1920/21. But, leaving capital punishment on one side, would it have made any real difference to Bailey's trial?

I have defended many criminals during my career at the Bar, and more than enough of them have been charged with murder. Reading a little about Bailey, and knowing something of his previous life and convictions, he comes across to me as a man who, once he found himself awaiting trial for murder, would have been looking at 'all the angles' whilst planning his defence.

He would not, today, have been facing the probability of execution if convicted, but nonetheless he would have been looking for a route that would avoid any lengthy prison sentence. He was a petty con man, who clearly believed that he could lie his way out of many difficulties in life.

In his note to the Coroner, he says, 'No blame attaches to the chemist. I could always bluff to attain my ends.' Until he faced the reality of the witness box, he probably believed that he could bluff his way out of trouble.

As with any defendant, it was up to Bailey to choose his own defence. His lawyers would advise him as to the law, but he would have to give them his account of what actually had happened, and how it was that his wife came to die. As it was, he was criticised at the trial, as he was bound to be, for changing his account so many times.

The one that he eventually decided upon – namely that his wife had done everything to herself, by herself, and that he had simply tried to save her – was really the only course that he could have taken to avoid conviction, bearing in mind the state of the law at the time, and the evidence that was stacked up against him, much of it by his own words in the note to the Coroner, and by what he had said to the police.

Today, a good Defence lawyer would have impressed upon Bailey that his best chance of avoiding a conviction for murder was to admit to being a part of a suicide pact. Suicide is no longer a crime, and aiding and abetting suicide is no longer murder.

On the evidence, the obvious line for him to take is that reflected by his note to the Coroner – namely, he had had a suicide pact with his wife, but that he had been arrested before he could go through with his side of the pact and kill himself. A guilty plea to aiding and abetting suicide, if accepted by the Prosecution, would probably only have brought a short prison sentence.

However, today, as in 1921, had such a plea been available, it is unlikely that upon the evidence available the Prosecution would have accepted such a plea and, further, Bailey would still have faced trial for the attempted rape of Miss Marks. His future would have been far from bright. Thus, although today Bailey should be given the advice that I set out above, it is unlikely in my opinion that he would take it.

He was the sort of man who would back himself to deceive others, and, if he could deceive the jury into believing that his wife had killed herself against his wishes, he would be acquitted of any crime in relation to her death. Murderers plotting to kill often lose touch with reality, and do not appreciate that their chance of getting away with their crime is slim. The same can be true once they are arrested and charged. There is a desire to clutch at straws and avoid reality.

Undoubtedly, today, a full, up-to-date psychiatric report on Bailey would have been obtained. Whatever the truth of his mental state, Bailey had a history of psychiatric illness as a youth, and there were suggested suicide attempts some years before. Psychiatry today is far in advance of where it was in 1921.

The prison service would want some form of psychiatric appraisal done on him to assess whether he was a suicide risk in custody, and his lawyers would have applied for a full report to be prepared for trial purposes. The Judge would almost certainly be persuaded that he would be assisted by one in the event of a conviction.

At Bailey's trial, it is clear that his Defence team eventually received instructions from him not to run insanity, even as a second-string defence. Reading the transcript of Bailey's evidence, and knowing something of his criminal past, I think that that was the right decision. No jury was going to find him insane.

However, had the modern defence of diminished responsibility been available in 1921, when execution threatened at the end of an unsuccessful trial, and with things looking very black [as they did for Bailey from the outset of his trial], a psychiatric report might just have saved Bailey's life. The fact that there was none available is surprising.

We do not know what instructions exactly Bailey gave to his solicitors and to his barrister on the topic, but, almost without exception, in modern times a report would have been available to the Court. At Bailey's trial, the evidence as to his mental state [or illness] was totally inadequate, and Johnston's attempts to persuade Professor Spilsbury to give an expert opinion were ill-founded and ill-advised.

However, even today, whether a psychiatric report would have suggested diminished responsibility is, I think, doubtful. One of the problems for Bailey was contained in his note to the Coroner, where he says, 'Please that God will forgive her. Forgive me … please God, Father of all nature, forgive us all.' He is there clearly expressing a sense of fault, and acknowledging that a suicide pact [as he claimed it was] was wrong.

In my opinion, as so often in a criminal trial, the real problem for Bailey was the evidence. It gave the Prosecution plenty of bricks with which to build their case. Mr Johnston, in his closing speech, conceded that his task was a 'somewhat difficult one', which indeed it was. Reading between the lines of the press reports of both his opening and closing speeches,

Mr Johnston seems always to have been very much 'on the back foot', struggling to find the persuasive arguments that his client needed to secure an acquittal.

The only record that appears to survive of Mr Young KC's closing speech is a report in the *Bucks Free Press* of 21 January 1921. The coverage in the press was, as is almost always the case even today, very pro–Prosecution, and clearly the paper was impressed by Mr Young KC's oratory. His 80 minutes of advocacy received the same number of column inches as Mr Johnston's 210 minutes.

Hugo Young KC was clearly a very experienced jury advocate of his time and, in all the circumstances, it appears that his contest with Mr Johnston was a hopeless mismatch.

For instance, before starting to deal in his speech with the evidence, Mr Young KC seems to have made an implied suggestion to the jury that Mr Johnston had taken far too long in his closing speech/presentation of the Defence, and that it had been his fault that it had not been possible to finish the case on Saturday [thus sparing them two extra days of confinement], making the point that, had they tried to finish on Saturday, he would not have risen to make his closing speech until 10.30pm [because, of course, of the length of the speech that they had just heard from Mr Johnston].

Having 'scathingly' [no doubt using that most powerful but unkind weapon of advocacy, sarcasm] dismissed the question of insanity, Mr Young KC illustrated for the jury the numerous lies that Bailey had told, and 'dramatically exclaimed that the prisoner's was the hand that gave the prussic acid to his wife'.

He ran through the evidence, and emphasised that, after Bailey's wife was dead, Bailey had not called for any assistance, did not contact a doctor or the police. Mr Young KC finished with the emotive words: '[Bailey] is a dangerous man, one who has a knowledge of drugs – a man who is a danger to the public – on the evidence adduced, you will have no hesitation in saying that he is guilty of the charge.' This line was no doubt designed to make the jury feel more comfortable at the prospect of a guilty verdict which would condemn Bailey to death.

Modern juries and Judges might well have found Mr Young KC's style overly dramatic or bombastic, but the points that he made on the evidence were good ones. Even though the law has changed, and the medical evidence, at least, would have been different, a prosecuting Queen's Counsel today might have addressed the jury in closing as follows:

'Bailey was tired of his unfortunate wife. She was six months pregnant with his second child, and had lost the bloom and shape of her youth. He was ten years older than her and had married her when she was still in her teens. He was prone to lust after younger, full-bodied women, and had clearly had enough of her.

'He carefully planned her murder, going to considerable lengths to obtain, by the use of lies, the necessary poison. His apparent obsession with a new system of recording music may in part be genuine, but he used it as a ruse to lure comely young ladies to his home. He arranged for a series of young ladies, all of an age for him to have lawful sex with them if they consented, to come to his house. He could not possibly have afforded to pay them the wages that he offered.

'On the afternoon of 29 September, a Miss Marks attended at Barn Cottage, and Bailey decided that he should invite her back to stay the night. No doubt he wished to have his evil way with her. The problem that stood in his way was his wife. Sending Miss Marks from the house for a few hours, he used that time to poison his wife and, once she was dead, to hide her body upstairs in a bedroom. It may well be that he intended also to murder his young daughter, another unwanted encumbrance on his future, but she, in the end, he spared.

'When Miss Marks returned, he sent her up to an adjoining bedroom, and later tried to have sexual intercourse with her against her wishes, while his dead wife's body lay still warm next door. Miss Marks courageously fought him off, and the next day complained to Reverend JD Allen, who came to Barn Cottage to confront the defendant. Bailey lied to Reverend Allen as he had to so many others before … and as he has to you.

'Then, knowing that the game was up, Bailey decided to spare the life of his child, and took her to his family in Swindon. In a period of hopelessness, he decided to take the coward's way out, and to commit suicide. In that state of mind, he wrote the note addressed to the Coroner, minimising but admitting some of his guilt.

'Then he lost his nerve, and thus was still alive when arrested by police in Reading. Subsequently, he has changed his story and lied in a desperate attempt to avoid the consequences of his actions. The truth is that this was a planned and ruthless killing of an unwanted wife, by a method that others might use to dispose of an unwanted dog or cat.'

In summary, I do not find the styles of the advocates

concerned, as can be discerned from the transcript of the evidence, so very different to those used today. A modern trial would have followed a similar format, but at a gentler pace.

The jurors would have their own copies of all the documents supplied to them. The evidence would have gone more slowly, and the sitting hours would have been shorter. This is done to make life easier for the jury and the defendant, who may not be used to sitting and concentrating for long periods of time.

The important point is that the evidence would have been much the same. Hugo Young KC would still have torn Bailey apart in cross-examination [as he undoubtedly did in 1921]. Juries can tell a lie as well today as they ever did. Some of the things that Bailey said were simply unbelievable.

As it appears on the transcript, the Judge's style of summing up is 'old-fashioned', but not unfair. He left the question of insanity to the jury, although he clearly encouraged them to dismiss it. He obviously did not believe Bailey, but left all questions of fact to the jury, as he had to.

His approach certainly would not have helped Bailey's case, but the Judge was entitled to sum up in the way that he did. However, I have to rely upon the transcript of the learned Judge's summing up. One of the difficulties with 'old-fashioned' Judges, a number of whom I appeared in front of in days gone by, is that what looks perfectly fair and balanced on paper can sound very different in Court.

I have sympathy with Johnston in his complaint that the Judge had been unbalanced in his summing up. He probably was, since it is so often a Judge's tone of voice or facial expression that makes the real impact during a summing up, and those are things that do not appear on a transcript. However, his directions in law [as it was then] were all correct, and Johnston fought an uphill, losing battle in the Court of Appeal.

It is interesting to note that the potential dangers of an irresponsible press arose in Bailey's trial, as they still do so often today. Of course, these days the dangers come not only from the press reporting inaccurately or inappropriately, but also from the Internet, and Bailey's trial was spared the latter problems.

When the *Bucks Free Press* published material that had not been put in evidence at the trial, the Judge, Mr Justice McCardie, threatened the press with contempt of Court if they did it again, but apparently took no other action. He simply commented, 'The jury have probably not seen the paper.' Apparently, both Mr Young KC and Mr Johnston were content to leave matters there.

In modern times, Bailey would have had the advantage of his Defence Counsel making the last speech. Furthermore, looking at the timing of the case, Johnston would probably have left the jury overnight on Monday with all of his points ringing in their ears. No modern Judge would start summing up at 5.00pm.

The jury would have been sent home after Johnston had finished, to hear the Judge's summing up next morning, and then to retire and consider their verdicts. The jurors would not have been confined over five days as this jury was. But again, would that have made any difference to Bailey's chances?

In my opinion, it would not. The jury would no doubt have taken longer to consider all that they had heard, but I find it difficult to see how their decision could have been different. If Bailey ran the same defence today, a jury would reach the same verdict. Bailey had lied too many times. The Prosecution case against him was powerful.

His defence was extremely difficult to believe. Even in modern times, it is unlikely that any medical defence could have succeeded – certainly not insanity, nor, in my lawyer's opinion, diminished responsibility.

The only real difference is that today Bailey would not have been hanged. He would have languished for many years in prison, with a recommendation that he serve perhaps a minimum of 20 years. If a psychiatric report had described him as dangerous to the public [as Mr Young KC claimed that he was], he might have served considerably longer.

One thing, however, is certain – he would have had plenty of time to prove whether or not his musical notation system really worked. As it was, his system died with him in March 1921.

APPENDIX II
COMPARING NOTES

While in prison in Oxford awaiting his trial, Bailey wrote out a large number of copies of his musical notation, all of which he forwarded to his solicitors. In the following letter, he tried to summarise his hopes and fears for the system, which he confidently believed might earn him some sort of artistic immortality, but that would later be described by an expert at Bucks Assizes as 'a grotesque absurdity'.

I have asked you to take control for me of 'Modern Notation' – my system of Staff Notation, my reason being that I want our child to be provided for – I can work for myself – and that your remuneration would be derived from the negotiation or control of this system.

Before writing down all that I claim for it, I must mention that I have tested it in every conceivable way (also for witnesses), and that I have also submitted it to a Doctor of Music [whom he named], whose reply I am waiting for, as I think it best that I should do all this before the trial, as I do not like the idea of publicity after the Assizes, where I am concerned. I think there is no need for me to point out that the possessor of the copyright, registered patent designs, and all rights universal, is financially assured. This system is more for the younger generation, and the future, with the present system becoming obsolete.

The present school could rapidly assimilate it, and where they now have ten pupils, and eight failing, they would have a hundred pupils, no drudgery, a pleasant task, and success with it all. It is the drudgery, complexity, perplexity, confusion, the years of patient study and money (even then resulting in but poor results from some), that make and induce would-be pupils, otherwise desirous of learning music, to give up in despair, disgust and disappointment.

The 'Thelwall' and 'Beeker' methods of 'learning for the pianoforte' are supposed to render learning the present system more agreeable. The 'Naunton System' is for the pianoforte only, and comparatively useless for the musical world. My system is a new 'Staff Notation', with the present, familiar appearance of clefs, Ornamentations, and Sings for performance retained, but no 'Sharps, Flats, Accidentals' or Naturals used, and the one Clef only used for any score, orchestral included.

It sounds preposterous, but the solution was so simple (I admit, an inspiration): keys are not even needed for performance; and the solving of one problem automatically led to the solving of the rest. It means uniformity of position of the notes, and never varying. The use of one Clef octave, instead of half a dozen, this one Clef embracing the compass of any Clef or desired range of compass. Simplicity, rapidity of tuition, pleasantness, brilliancy, efficiency, and easy sight reading for all; music and instruments learned in a mere fraction of the time now taken; for the masses; the ordinary intelligent; not difficult feats of memory and acumen for the talented few.

The old school have for centuries been striving for uniformity, with simplicity, with complete failure; the present system is still so completely bound up in intricacies, the accumulated modifyings of the past, and yet antagonism, prejudice, and conservatism, is still prevalent.

Jennie-Helen Moston, MA (Cantab), PGDip. (Hons), LRSM, is a professional accompanist, teacher and examiner for the Associated Board of the Royal Schools of Music. She studied at Chetham's School of Music, Manchester; St John's College, Cambridge; and at the Guildhall School of Music and Drama in London.

Having examined Bailey's 'Modern Notation', she is able to provide us with an expert's viewpoint:

Bailey believed with the utmost confidence that he had invented a revolutionary musical notation system that would be, in his own words, 'for the masses: the ordinary intelligent'. He wrote that 'it [sounds] preposterous, but the solution [to the future of musical notation] was so simple (I admit, an inspiration)'.

He was aiming for 'simplicity with uniformity', to avoid the 'dreadful monotony, harassing perplexities [and] the difficulties ...' that was posed by the traditional system of musical notation. Ultimately, he asserted that his system would simplify sight-reading for all and that it would be possible to learn to read music and to play instruments 'in a mere fraction of the time ...'

And so it appears that Bailey himself struggled to grasp the traditional form of notation and therefore sought to find other ways, loosely based on the traditional system, to notate music. Unfortunately, after studying his numerous sketchings, musings, formal treatises and letters to his solicitors, it quickly becomes clear just how his invention that sounded so promising has lain forgotten for the best part of a century.

The reason is, quite simply, that his system was fatally flawed. While Bailey was trying in earnest to improve the lives of the next generation of musicians – he insisted that 'this system is more for the younger generation, and the future, with the present system becoming obsolete' – he did not realise the fundamental weakness in his system: that his 'new system' could only ever have been employed (if we ignore the other inconsistencies about which I shall write shortly) for music written for piano; music that is written using the usual two stave set-up, one for right hand, one for left hand.

He himself, in a letter written to his solicitors Messrs RS Wood and Co, ironically acknowledges that methods of learning written specifically for the piano (such as the 'Naunton System') are 'comparatively useless to the musical world'.

The reason why his system would only have worked for a two-hand piano piece is because he does not specify with the use of different clefs (treble clef; bass clef; C clefs – such as the alto or tenor clef) at which *octave* (pitch) the notes should be played, i.e. in layman's terms, the C that is known as 'middle C' in traditional notation ('the old system' as he so called it) – which lies underneath the treble clef on its own ledger line or above the bass clef on its own ledger line – is only recognisable in Bailey's system by lying *between* these two staves.

Bailey, in fact, only uses one 'clef', which enables 'uniformity of position of the notes. The use of one clef octave, instead of half a dozen, the one clef embracing the compass of any clef or desired range of compass.' However, while this is true – B always lies just below the dotted line thus making the notes instantly recognisable – this also means that it is never clear which octave the note written should be played – how high or how low – if only one stave is used.

Therefore, despite Bailey believing an orchestral score could be notated using his system, it would be completely impossible. The individual players would be able to recognise the note names (A, E, G, etc.), but not at which octave the note should be played.

It seems that he subconsciously knew that different clefs were necessary to signify which was the lower stave of the two, for some examples do show the lower clef with a 'tail'. However, this is inconsistent – sometimes the tail is missing entirely; sometimes Bailey adds further confusion by writing the clef upside down!

Throughout his handwritten work, mistakes are commonplace. For example, for those with some knowledge of traditional notation, the order of sharps and flats appear in the wrong order, over the incorrect lines of the stave; clefs are placed over the wrong lines of the stave; notes are not aligned correctly; and ironically, in examples translating from 'old' to 'new' systems, he even makes mistakes notating the correct notes in his own system!

The importance of clefs goes further than just to imply the pitch of a note. Not only do they show where the semitones and tones lie on the stave, they also allow the avoidance of ledger lines (extra lines written above or below the staves). For example, when a passage for cello encompasses unusually high notes, rather than being written in the bass clef (the lowest clef), the music would be written in the tenor clef whose stave covers higher pitches. Bailey's system uses many more ledger lines, which, on a visual level, is more complicated to read and appears more cluttered aesthetically.

The layout and clarity of musical notation is extremely important – the simpler the font and the cleaner the page, the better. The majority of musicians must sight-read as an integral part of their music making. In order to do this, one needs to see the patterns of intervals (distances between notes) quickly.

Even if we disregard the importance of clefs, patterns are easily recognisable in traditional notation because notes are either written on lines or spaces of the stave. They relate especially clearly to the notes of a keyboard instrument, for the pattern of consecutive notes on the piano directly correlates to consecutive notes on the music, sitting on a line, then a space, line, space, etc.

Therefore, if three notes lie on three adjacent lines of the music, three notes on the piano are played with a gap in between (that relates to the three spaces on the music). With Bailey's added dotted line in the middle of the stave, it *is* immediately clear where B and C are (as mentioned above), but not where the adjacent notes are as in traditional notation (because notes never lie on this dotted, middle line of the stave), thus making the immediate recognition of intervals unclear.

Flats and sharps, double flats and double sharps are intrinsically linked to the musical language in which pieces are written. Composers have always chosen a key in which to write a piece, using keys that suit the technical abilities of an instrument, the mood of the piece, or the subtleties of the poetry in a song, for example.

Romantic composers went so far as to hide messages in pieces through the use of specific keys. Within this idea lies the ability to then lead *to* or distance oneself *from* other keys – and this therefore requires accidentals (sharps or flats) that either belong to the home harmonies or push away from them.

Bailey naïvely believed that 'keys are not needed for performance'. He disposes of the use of all sharps and flats, and settles for a single 'note raised'. For instruments that do not have fixed intonation (such as stringed instruments or voices, for example), this is a disaster.

String quartets, for example, tune to a consonant sound dependent on the key. Take a C sharp in the chord of A major that typically leads as chord V to its chord I of D major. This C sharp would be far sharper than a D flat (its enharmonic equivalent – i.e. they are the 'same' pitch) in a B flat minor chord that requires a minor 3rd interval between B flat and D flat to really underpin the harmony.

As excited as he is by not using key signatures, he attempts, however, to notate these by placing a sign on the note according to the key in which it is. This is completely redundant, for the key signature relates directly to the established intervals within the octave that make up the traditional scale (major or minor) and its key signature which Bailey so naïvely disregards!

Our Western system of notation has been embellished and developed over literally thousands of years, and has actually remained virtually unchanged for several centuries. It is by no means the only notation that is in use today – in fact, many 20th-century composers have modified the system better to indicate the instruments' requirements that are not possible to notate in this traditional system.

Bailey was not the first, and will not be the last, to attempt to reform the way we notate music, and we, as musicians, must be ready to learn and appreciate alternative forms of notation.

Therefore, I will thank him for attempting to make life easier for those who read music but, unfortunately, he failed the music that he was notating on so many fronts that it is no surprise that his ideas have been confined to the realms of history.

ACKNOWLEDGEMENTS

To date, I have written books about both the living and the dead, but, whether they were alive and kicking at the time or firmly interred, my research always managed to include some, in many cases much, first-hand witness of the subjects in question, be they actors, a writer, director, or a film and television mogul.

Venturing for the first time into the world of true-life crime and, to boot, one that was committed fully 90 years ago, there was little likelihood of my being able to speak directly to any of the principals involved. However, as you will have read earlier, I was lucky at least to have met one of the key players, albeit a passive participant, in this tragedy. At the time of our meeting, though, writing a book about the fateful life and times of her parents was perhaps the furthest thing from my mind when we did have our brief encounter nearly 30 years ago.

This is an opportunity then belatedly to acknowledge Hollie and also, from much more recent acquaintance, kind members from two further generations of her surviving family who agreed to speak to me but asked that their anonymity be respected.

My deepest thanks are reserved for Richard Tedham, a cricketing colleague and friend for more than 40 years, whose skills, in this case as an enthusiastic local historian and dogged researcher, proved quite invaluable. Grateful thanks also to another old friend, Brian Lett QC, an author in his own right, who kindly provided a fascinating contemporary view and commentary about this historic case; to professional musician and teacher Jennie-Helen Moston, who contributed a hugely valuable modern-day insight into thwarted musical ambitions; to John Blake who kindly indulged a first attempt at True Crime, and to his colleague, my editor, Sara Cywinski, who carefully nursed it through to completion; Jane Judd, my agent; to Michael Eagleton and Ken Townsend, two veteran and extremely knowledgeable local historians, also prolific collectors of postcards, who generously helped me with my picture research; and to Steve Cohen, Editor of the *Bucks Free Press*, who gave me kind permission to quote extensively from 1920 and 1921 editions of his newspaper, as well as from the *BFP* publication *No Fear Nor Favour!* by the late Bob Perrin, including the reproduction of photographs.

Then there were all the national and regional archives I plundered for reports and pictures, and, particularly in the case of Kew, extensive Home Office files on the case including some key trial exhibits. So thanks, in no particular order, to: Adrian Ailes and all the staff at the National Archives, Kew; Celia Pilkington, Inner Temple Archivist; Jen Booth, Old Rossallian Society; Chris Hawkins, Oxfordshire

Record Office; Thomas Knollys & Clare Hopkins, as well as the President and Fellows of Trinity College, Oxford; Mike Dewey, archivist of the *Bucks Free Press*; His Honour Judge Tyler, Resident Judge, & Helen Hemingway, Court Clerk, Aylesbury Crown Court; Eveleen Rooney, Westminster Reference Library; Alan Pinnock, *Daily Mail* Pictures; Solo Syndication; Andre Gailani, the *Punch* archive; Local Studies Library, Nottingham; Darren Over, Ministry of Justice; Teresa Gorecka, *Nottingham Post*; Sarah Donbavand, Civil Section Manager, Taunton County Court; Graeme Edwards, Somerset Heritage Centre; Richard Durack, Newham Archives and Local Studies Library; Stratford Library; General Register Office, Southport, Merseyside; Kate Brolly, Library Customer Services Officer, Camden Local Studies & Archives Centre; Andrew Bell, Home Office Press; Skip Walker, Editor *Wilts & Gloucestershire Standard*; Roger Bettridge, Bucks County Archivist; Ellie Stokes & Staff at Oxford Castle and Oxford Malmaison (formerly Oxford Prison), notably, the duty manager who showed me where the 'execution suite' used to be situated; British History Online; WPS, High Wycombe & Marlow; The Meteorological Office; Anne Bradley, Archivist – Bristol Record Office; *Maidenhead Advertiser*; *Bucks Herald*; *Bucks Advertiser and Aylesbury News*; *Daily Express*; various websites, but in particular www.ancestry.co.uk, www.freebmd.org.uk and www.findmypast.co.uk; Wycombe, Maidenhead and Aylesbury Libraries, especially the Local Studies Departments and County Archives; Gloria Barclay, Clerk to, and Barbara Wallis, member of, Little Marlow Parish Council; and the incredibly accommodating staff at the Newspaper Library, Colindale.

Grateful acknowledgement to the following books and

their authors: *The Book of Marlow* by AJ (Jock) Cairns (Baron Birch, 1994); *Buckinghamshire Tales of Murder & Mystery* by David Kidd-Hewitt (Countryside Books, 2003); *Murder in Buckinghamshire* by Len Woodley (Saga, 1994); *The New Murderers' Who's Who* by JHH Gaute and Robin Odell (Harrap, 1989); *Judicial Wisdom of Mr Justice McCardie*, edited by Albert Crew (Ivor Nicholson & Watson, 1932); *Diary of a Hangman* by John Ellis (True Crime Library, 2000); *Lethal Witness* by Andrew Rose (Tempus, 2007); *Social Conditions in Britain 1918–1939* by Stephen Constantine (Methuen, 1983).

Thanks to the following individuals who helped with extra research and suggestions: Ben Wilson; Isobel Mackenzie; Sue Norton; Tim Green; Anwar Brett; Anne Reid; William Scott; Dr Roger Moston; Marney Wilson; Paul Brown Constable.

Finally, to neighbour and good friend Bernard Burger, who welcomed us into his home providing warmth and wi-fi while builders spent several winter months rebuilding and refurbishing our new home in the village following a 'downsize' move from 'the scene of the crime' in the summer of 2011.

Little Marlow, 2012